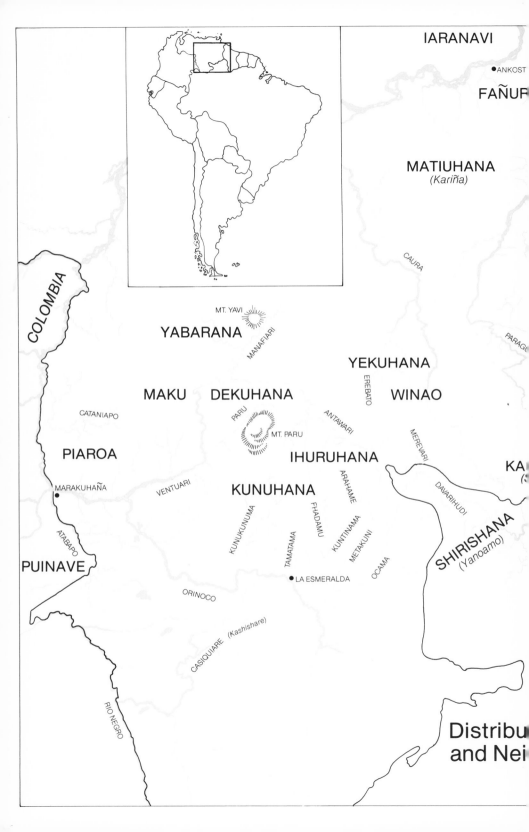

DAMA
(Caribbean Sea)

HURUNKU

CUYUNI

● AMENADIÑA

MAZARUNI

AUYAN TEPUI

GUYANA
VENEZUELA

Ë'TI
(Arekuna)

RONI

DODOIMA
(Mt. Roraima)

ESSEQUIBO

Ë'TI
(Makushi)

MARACA ISLAND

RUPUNUNI

KANUKU MTS.

BRAZIL

BRANCO

MATIUHANA
(Kariña)

the Makiritare
g Tribes

North Point Press
San Francisco
1980

WATUNNA

An Orinoco Creation Cycle

Marc de Civrieux

edited and translated by David M. Guss

WATUNNA was originally published in a different version under the title, WATUNNA: MITOLOGÍA MAKIRITARE, Monte Avila Editores C.A., Caracas, 1970.

Selections have previously appeared in Parabola and Zero to whom grateful acknowledgment is made.

Title page photograph: The *atta,* the first of which was built by Wanadi as a replica of the universe.

Glyphs and maps were drawn by Rose Craig.

Table of Contents

A Teller's Preface

The first *Watunna*—a somewhat different one from this—was initially published in Caracas, Venezuela in 1970. It had taken Marc de Civrieux more than twenty years to piece together, returning to the villages of the Kunukunuma year after year to listen to the many Makiritare who gave him the hundreds of fragments and episodes which were eventually woven together to form the whole. For this is the *Watunna* told daily, not the ritual *Watunna* of festival, but the one told every day in bits and pieces as time and need demand. And so there was not one informant, but many, and when in the end he had taken all the versions and given them the order they would have if there were just one speaker and one occasion, he changed roles and became the teller himself. The tables were suddenly turned and the investigator began giving the stories back to the people:

> Surprised and delighted, they gathered around to listen, correcting and adding new details as they were needed. When some episode had been misplaced, they signalled: "No. That comes before." Or: "It comes later." When something had been forgotten, they said: "Here, you're missing this little piece," and went on to relate it. And so the 'montage' was approved and became an entirely spontaneous, collective collaboration. And Makiritare came from all over to ask to hear it and each time, large, excited crowds of people would sit down to listen, interrupting every so often to offer their advice or criticism.

And so the *Watunna*, a word derived from the verb *adeu*, which means 'to tell', became just that, another telling, which is in the end what the translation of any oral tradition must become if it is to remain alive. I learned this when I brought the *Watunna* into English, for this too was more than a straight word for word translation. It was another telling—the first one coming into English. And so it is my

vii

hope that each reading of these tales may also become a telling and that they all live with the same force and meaning with which they were spoken by their first tellers, the Makiritare of the Upper Orinoco.

I was fortunate enough to be able to hear many of these tales while living with the Makiritare for different periods of time between 1976 and 1978. I was also extremely fortunate to be able to undertake the translation of the *Watunna* while in close collaboration with Marc de Civrieux, without whose help this work could not have been completed. It was through this enchanted alliance that we were able to make the various additions and improvements which have been included in the present edition. This work, along with the time spent in the Headwater Place, Ihuruña, would never have been possible without the generous support of the Organization of American States, The Explorers Club, and The Marsden Foundation. To all three, and to Dr. Elizabeth M. Bonbright who directs the latter, I wish to extend my most heartfelt gratitude.

David M. Guss
Venice, California
1980

Watunna

INTRODUCTION

THE PEOPLE

The Makiritare live, as they did at the time of the Spanish Conquest, on the right or northern bank of the Upper Orinoco River of Venezuela. This region of mountains and virgin forest has remained almost unexplored up to this day. It is crossed by five great rivers, all tributaries of the Orinoco itself—the Kunukunuma, Iguapo, Padamo, Upper Ventuari, and Upper Caura.

The name Makiritare is not their own, but the one the Spanish conquistadors gave them in 1759, the year of their first contact. These pioneers had as their guides and interpreters a group of Arawak-speaking Indians who used to trade with a tribe they referred to as Makiritare. It was under this name that the first detachment of Spaniards heard of them. The guides were Uaipunabi (Puinavis) and Urumanavi Indians from the Atabapo River. The name Makiritare, of Arawak origin, stuck and has been used in Venezuela without interruption ever since.

In 1912, a German ethnographer, Theodor Koch-Grünberg, visited Makiritare living in the headwaters of the Caura (Merevari) and Ventuari, but he gave them the name Mayonkong, the same as their eastern neighbors, the Arekuna and Taulipang, give them. Koch-Grünberg arrived there from the Mt. Roraima plains and Uraricoera headwaters to the east. It's obvious that his first news of the Makiritare, under the name Mayonkong, must have come from these eastern informants. But Koch-Grünberg also referred to a subdivision of the tribe into four local groups known to themselves as Ihuruhana (those from the Caura, Ventuari, and Padamo headwaters), Dekuhana (those from Mt. Dekuhana, the mythic birthplace of the tribe), Yekuhana (a phonetic variant of the preceding name), and Kunuhana (those from the Kunu or Kunukunuma River). The Dekuhana and Yekuhana were originally one group. Then, as their population grew, they split into two separate bands with their own chiefs and communal organizations. Mt. Dekuhana (or Yekuhana), from which all the Makiritare are said to originate, is located in Ihuruña, an area formed by the headwaters of the major rivers of that region. The Dekuhana, Yekuhana, and Kunuhana all emigrated from this mythic site of communal origin where the Ihuruhana ('Headwater People') still live today. The four groups are closely tied to each other by the same oral tradition, the *Watunna*, the sacred cornerstone of their political and commercial alliance. They also all speak the language of So'to, and for that reason, they form the So'to tribe. If one wishes to use the Makiritare's own name to refer to them, it is this: So'to.*

The *Watunna* is the compendium of religious and social models of the 'true people' or So'to. These are the sacred deeds and actions of the heroes in primordial times. These four local groups all speak the language of So'to, the same one which the first heroes of the *Watunna* spoke and taught. So'to literally means 'people', 'man', 'human being', but the use of the word is restricted to those people who speak a common language united by their collective origin. Those who do not speak that language or do not know the *Watunna* are considered animals. The word So'to also means 'twenty' as this is the number of fingers and toes a human has. It serves as the natural basis for the indigenous counting system and is also the symbol for man.

For the Makiritare, the term So'to has a purely linguistic significance. The native concept of tribe is not a racial one. The tribe does at various times adopt members of other tribes, principally women and children, and as they live with the tribe and learn the So'to language, they become So'to. So'to, the member of the tribe or the true human being, is recognized by his manner of speaking and not by his physical form. Makiritare mythology is filled with examples of beings considered nonhuman (animals, invisible spirits, shamans, demons of all sorts) who, in order to fool people, magically change their forms and adopt that of the So'to. Any species of being can alter its form, but it is language which identifies it. The apparently 'human' tribes which

---

*Some modern ethnographers have substituted the name Makiritare for that of Dekuana or Yekuana to designate the tribe, avoiding the traditional usage of the first name. This is not a solution however, as Dekuana and Yekuana are no more than two of the four local groupings of the tribe. So'to remains the only true autogenous name for the Makiritare.

speak languages unintelligible to the So'to actually belong to the non-human category. These tribes will occasionally take on fictitious forms, but their strange language will always reveal their true nature. These beings are the enemies of the real people and can be hunted like animals. The influence of this linguistic factor can be seen in the instinctive distrust of the So'to toward all foreign tribes (human animals) as well as in their choice of commercial and military alliances. There is no doubt that their linguistic affinity with the eastern Cariban tribes (the Arekuna, Taulipang, and Makushi) who dwell in the plains of Mt. Roraima and the Uraricoera basin, has led to their traditionally excellent relations. These eastern groups are members of the single great Pemon tribe whom the So'to call Ë'ti. The word Pemon, like So'to, means 'human being', 'the one who speaks Pemon', and the number 'twenty'. The concept of tribe, both proper and foreign, is the same among both groups. Their respective languages allow the two a close cultural and commercial relationship which is explained in each of their oral traditions. Each one, So'to and Pemon, is almost human for the other.

As the linguistic difference between two tribes becomes more pronounced, the mutual communications become more problematic. A tribe whose language is unintelligible is dangerous to the 'real human'. A typical example is that of the Makiritare's habitual enemy in the times of the Conquest as recalled in the oral tradition. These were the True Caribs who call themselves Kariña. For these people too, their name means 'human being', 'one who speaks Kariña' and the number 'twenty'. Despite representing the original trunk from which the various Cariban tribes branched out, the True Carib has a difficult language for these other tribes to understand. Beyond the evident morphological nexus, the Kariña's phonetics differ significantly from those of the So'to and Pemon, creating a major barrier to communication. During the Spanish Conquest, missionaries noted the same problem among the True Caribs and the Cariban Shoto of northeastern Venezuela. They wrote that these languages were completely distinct and that the Caribans could not understand the Caribs.

The Kariña were warlike and proud of their tribe, considering themselves as the only true human beings. Numerous, powerful, and almost invincible in war, they made no distinctions between the Caribans, Arawaks, and linguistically independent tribes. To them, all foreigners were unintelligible barbarians, dangerous animals to be hunted and destroyed. The Carib incursions into neighboring territories were actual hunting expeditions. The Kariña practiced ritual cannibalism and they ate, for magical purposes, the flesh of their victims, whom they did not consider human. These rites communicated the occult power of their enemies' souls, whose flesh was ingested as a powerful spirit food.

At the time of the Conquest, the Makiritare were the True Caribs' immediate neighbors, sharing with them the Caura watershed. The border between the two tribes was Para Falls where navigation of the river was cut in half. The Kariña would invade up river, raiding the Makiritare villages along the Merevari, Canaracuni and Erebato Rivers. They took prisoners and traded them with their Dutch allies on the Essequibo in exchange for guns, metal utensils and other European goods. When, in 1775, the Spaniards finally succeeded in dislodging these marauders of the Orinoco and lower Caura, the Kariña invaded the Makiritare territories in the Caura headwaters and from there fled to the Uraricoera River and Mt. Kanuku, where they went on trading with the Dutch miners and merchants who offered them protection.

The Makiritare gave these Carib enemies the name Matiuhana. Continually suspect of black magic, they feared them greatly. This is why so many tales appear in the *Watunna* portraying Carib shamans in the form of jaguars and Kanaima monsters out looking for people to eat.

THE HISTORY

For this people without a history, living in an endless Stone Age for thousands of years in the virgin forests of the Upper Orinoco, their first contact with the conquistadors was an extraordinary event. The impact of this event on the psyches of these tribes can be felt in the *Watunna*. The Makiritare, through their repulsion of the foreign invader, escaped the Conquest. The Spaniards' attempt to subjugate them and save their souls ended in failure. Belated and brief, it took place in the second half of the eighteenth century, in the last years of the colonial era and lasted but two decades. The memory of that chaotic period, both miraculous and disastrous, has not disappeared from the epic tales of the *Watunna*.

Up until 1744, no Spaniard had even tried to enter the Upper Orinoco. It was a sacred sanctuary guarded by impenetrable walls of water—a no man's land. Atures and Maipures Falls were inhospitable obstacles to navigation. But in this year, a Spanish explorer, daring the unknown, skirted the falls and charted his course up river to the high Orinoco. His name was Manuel Roman and he was the Father Superior of the Orinoco River's Jesuit Missions. He was chosen to live an extraordinary adventure which he himself would hardly believe. In this no man's land, he happened across some European traders who were very calmly paddling down the Orinoco without the slightest idea of where they were. They claimed to be subjects of the Portuguese Crown out exploring their king's dominions in the Indies. They insisted they were on some tributary of the Amazon River, as they had arrived there by water from that river. Refusing to believe the Spanish Jesuit's claims that they were on the Orinoco, the errant Lusitanians allowed Roman to join them on their return voyage. He travelled with them as far as the Amazon, and thus confirmed the existence of a connection with the Orinoco. Then he went back and told the Spanish, but no one in the entire Indies would believe him. Nevertheless, the Spanish Crown was anxious about reports of Portuguese incursions in the headwaters of the Orinoco. In order to verify these, and take defensive measures, the king quickly dispatched a Frontier Commission under the charge of the Marquis José Solano with an order to confirm or disprove the mysterious fluvial connection of the Casiquiare channel and to explore all the unknown lands of the Upper Orinoco and Rio Negro.

The Marquis and his men crossed Atures and Maipures Falls in 1756 and installed their headquarters in a place they called San Fernando de Atabapo where a group of Puinave Indians were living. The discovery expedition lasted a full six years, till 1761. Makiritare legend still recalls San Fernando de Atabapo (Marakuhaña) as the place where Iaranavi, the European discoverer, had his home.

In the *Watunna,* the figure of the Spanish conquistador is separated into two contradictory images, one luminous, the other dark, incarnations of two antagonistic characters, Iaranavi and Fañuru. Iaranavi, the White Man, corresponds to the Golden Legend of the Discovery. The *Watunna* identifies him with the great egret, that beautiful, pure bird who symbolizes light. It tells that Iaranavi was good, rich, wise, powerful, and generous. He was also the master of that marvellous metal, iron, and the master of the *arakusa* (arcabuz), that invincible weapon which the *Watunna* identifies with the heavenly power of thunder and lightning. Like the Makiritare, Iaranavi was a creature of Wanadi, the celestial father of all Being. Fañuru (a phonetic alteration of Español, 'Spanish') on the other hand, represents the Black Legend of the Conquest. He was an evil cannibal who raided distant lands killing and enslaving Indians. Not satisfied with overrunning the So'to, he abused Wanadi and eventually forced him to leave his home on the Earth. Fañuru's memory is engraved on the consciousness of the So'to as a synonym for the devil. Even today, shamanic rites conjure up the name of Fañuru along with those of other evil spirits in order to keep his malevolent force away from the sick and their homes.

The period from 1759 to 1767 was the 'Epoch of Iaranavi'. Later, according to the *Watunna,* another, less joyous, period came. This was that of the demon, Fañuru, from 1767 to 1776. During this second period, the initial Spanish-Makiritare idyl rapidly deteriorated. Iaranavi was deposed by a devil. Finally, a Makiritare rebellion burst out, led by a powerful shaman who freed the Indians from their new oppressors.

Iaranavi appears for the first time in Makiritare territory in the year 1759 under the form of Sergeant Francisco Fernandez de Bobadilla and a detachment of soldiers. Sent from San Fernando de Atabapo by the Marquis Solano, they explore the Iguapo, Kunukunuma, and Padamo Rivers situated by the strategic Orinoco-Casiquiare fork. The Iaranavi receive a warm welcome from the village of Warapa, located to the east of Mt. Duida between the Iguapo and Lower Padamo. Soon after, they visit another village called Warema (for its chief) in the Upper Padamo beyond the mouth of the Kuntinamo on the banks of the Kuitamoni. In order to reach it, these unknown children of Wanadi had to go up the Padamo to Cuare Rapids and then follow two more tributaries, the Machakuri and Mawanami, up river. It was a dangerous journey through difficult mountainous terrain. Accepted into the Makiritare's homes, the Iaranavi promised the So'to protection against their enemies. They exchanged fabulous gifts for their food and left, promising to return.

In the beginning of the following year, the Iaranavi came back. This time their leader was Lieutenant Apolinar Diez de la Fuente, another official from Marakuhaña. He told Chief Warema and his people that he had come to defend them against the marauding Caribs who were invading their lands in search of prisoners to sell as slaves. They were also going to defend them against the Portuguese who were infiltrating

from the Amazon by way of the Casiquiare. In exchange for this protection, the Iaranavi chief asked for Warema's loyalty as a vassal of his
Catholic king and demanded that his people convert to Christianity.
As a token, Warema changed the name of his village to Santa Gertrudiz.

The king of Spain had ordered the Iaranavi to build a fort at the
mouth of the Casiquiare to protect the So'to. This fort was to be built
immediately and called Buenaguardia. The Iaranavi invited their new
allies to move to the banks of the Orinoco, near the Christian fort in
order to benefit from its protection and the trade offered by the Spanish merchants.

Don Apolinar also told Warema that the Iaranavi wanted to take
advantage of the Upper Padamo's wild cocoa. Warema told him that
there was indeed lots of cocoa in the mountains which he would lead
them to. The Makiritare and Spanish set off together to explore this
land of promise. The people of Warema collected sixty baskets of cocoa, for which Don Apolinar gave them iron, cloth, and other goods.
The alliance was sealed with a great feast.

The Iaranavi left and Don Apolinar began supervising the building
of the Buenaguardia fort. Then he explored the adjoining territory
around the foot of Mt. Duida and discovered along the Orinoco an
ideal plain for the founding of a new village where he planned to
gather the people of Warapa and Warema together. The plain was
close to Buenaguardia and the mouth of the Iguapo where Warema
had a port for canoes, from which he controlled the commerce along
the Upper Orinoco. Don Apolinar called this new site La Esmeralda.
He had discovered veins and seams of beautiful transparent rock crystals there. The So'to called them *wiriki* and their shamans put them in
their maracas to give them their magic power. The Iaranavi thought
that the crystals were emeralds and that the deposits also contained
gold. Eventually hoping to turn La Esmeralda into an El Dorado to
refinance the Conquest, Don Apolinar wanted to make the Indians
exploit these mines. The Iaranavi craved gold, while the So'to dreamed
of nothing but the Iaranavi's iron. For Don Apolinar, the El Dorado of
La Esmeralda would be a mine filled with precious stones and gold.
For the people of Warema and Warapa, Meraraña (the *Watunna*'s
name for La Esmeralda) would be the El Dorado of the Indians, a
place where they could get all the Iaranavi iron they desired. The exchange of iron for gold was the incentive for this alliance between In-

dian and Spaniard. They were both looking for Heaven, but searching for it in the earth.

Solano had instructed Don Apolinar to discover the mysterious sources of the Orinoco River. The Iaranavi believed that Manoa, the fantastic City of Gold, was hidden on the shores of a mythical lake named Parimé which was to be found in the uncharted headwaters of the Orinoco and Uraricoera. A Makiritare trader named Une (or Iune) was enticed by the Iaranavi fantasy and agreed to accompany them up river, warning them, however, that they could not reach the sources of the Orinoco due to the many rapids and savage Shirishana Indians who dwelled there. Upon reaching Guaharibos Rapids, Don Apolinar suddenly announced that he had discovered the sources of the great river and turned around, having come nowhere near his goal.

Soon after, the Iaranavi sent soldiers to the villages of Warapa and Warema to bring the Indians to Meraraña where they would erect a great village. The So'to enthusiastically left in November of 1760 and began to build it. But this initial joy soon turned to cruel disillusion for both the So'to and the Iaranavi as the project was abruptly abandoned. The village of Meraraña was left unfinished. Don Apolinar and his troops were recalled from La Esmeralda and the So'to forced to return to their former villages, once more exposed to the Caribs. The fort at Buenaguardia and the headquarters at Marakuhaña were also abandoned. By the year 1761, Solano, the commander in chief of the Iaranavi, had concluded his exploratory mission. The king had ordered him to gather all his troops, concentrating them on the strategic Lower Orinoco where they were to build a city-fort capable of securing all of Spanish Guyana against the traffic of the Caribs and Dutch.

It was four years before the So'to received news of the Iaranavi again. This was in 1764, a crucial year in the history of Spanish Guyana. Along the Orinoco, the Spanish had never had a military strength capable of defending their small forts and missions against the raids of the Caribs. Nevertheless, several small groups of Europeans had managed to maintain themselves there under the most extreme misery and danger. Now Solano was given material forces sufficient to impose the law of Iaranavi on the Orinoco. He chose a strategic site at the Angostura ('Narrows') of the river to raise his fort and so in 1764, that city which the Makiritare still call Ankosturaña (Angostura, the old name for present day Ciudad Bolivar) was founded.

Warema, the chief of the Upper Padamo's So'to, was to see Iaranavi's new fortress for himself. Bobadilla was sent out again to renew his contacts and solemnly invite Chief Warema, in the name of the king of Spain, to visit Ankosturaña. It was an unforgettable journey. Warema was able to view, with his own eyes, the El Doradõ dreamed of by the So'to, the 'City of Iron'. As Warema had believed, Ankosturaña was the source of the 'Riches of Heaven' which the Great Father Wanadi had given to Iaranavi, his chosen son, as a reward for his goodness and wisdom. He stared at the wealth, witnessed the feverish activity of the carpenters and masons, observed how they made their houses and their roofs of red tiles. He marvelled at Iaranavi's cows and his horses. Along with other chiefs from the Orinoco, he was received by the city's governor, Don Sabas Moreno de Mendoza. As tribute to his loyalty to the king of Spain, the Makiritare brought an offering of cocoa from the Padamo. He left loaded down with the honors and gifts owing to a chief. When he returned to his village of Santa Gertrudiz, he carried with him a canoe filled with treasures from Ankosturaña. The So'to gathered from every neighboring village to hear his tales. They never tired of listening to them. And so was born the story of that Earthly Paradise, Ankosturaña, which is still told today to every new generation of Makiritare.

Within two years, the city of Ankosturaña was flourishing. The ambitious new governor of Guyana, Manuel Centurión, decided to continue the conquest of the Orinoco, expel the Dutch-backed Caribs and renew the search for the mythic city of Manoa. José Solano, who was overseeing Centurión's activities from the capital in Caracas, ordered Don Apolinar to Guyana to resettle the abandoned village of La Esmeralda with the Makiritare. This would be the ideal advance post to control the movements of the Caribs and Dutch. The Makiritare would also help explore the supposed mines of precious stones and gold. It would be necessary to open a road straight through the forest between Angostura and La Esmeralda. It would follow the route of the Caribs and stop their raids on the Makiritare. It would be a base of operations in the search for El Dorado.

Now the Andalusian Capuchins wanted a part in this great scheme, but Centurión refused to let them participate. Nevertheless, the priests obtained control over all future missions in the Upper Orinoco and Rio Negro from Solano, the supreme commander in Caracas. In 1765, four of them left from Cabruta on the Middle Orinoco. Their prefect, Father Jerez de los Caballeros, wanted to convert the Makiritare himself. He put his companions in charge of founding the missions on the Rio Negro and set off alone for the Padamo where he planned to start a Christian village. Warema, remembering the failure five years earlier, refused, and the priest was forced to withdraw.

Two years later, Apolinar Diez de la Fuente visited Warema with a military force in order to invite him and his people to settle at La Esmeralda once again. The Makiritare ignored him. Against their will, the soldiers carried off several groups of Indians, and brought them to La Esmeralda where they were forced to build a dozen huts. This outrage was to mark the end of the epoch of Iaranavi. It began that of Fañuru.

In August, Father Jerez de los Caballeros arrived and began converting by force. Thus began the Meraraña mission mentioned in the *Watunna*. There the So'to found out for the first time who the Fadre (*Padres*, 'Fathers') were. This is where the legend presenting the missionaries as demons in the service of Fañuru began. The militant proselytism and intolerant messianism of the Catholics trampled over the So'to's religious tradition, forbidding its rites and ancient cults. The Makiritare were confined to Meraraña where they were forced to live with other tribes also kidnapped and deported to that mosquito-ridden plain. Father Jerez's mission did not last beyond three and a half months. Nevertheless, its brief duration left an indelible mark on the oral tradition of the Makiritare. He was implacably fanatical in his zealousness for salvation. At the same time as he spoke of the crucifixion of Christ, he pleaded for the destruction of Wanadi, the Makiritare's 'false god' who would be replaced by the religion of Jesus. The *Watunna* remembers this evangelism with bitterness. It states that the Fadre took Wanadi to Caracas, the Fañuru's city, to be crucified, and that they then tried to convince the So'to that they had killed him. But the *Watunna* says that this was a lie. Wanadi had too much power. He couldn't be killed. He was able to escape from those demons. Yet because of them, he was forced to say goodby to the Earth and flee to Heaven. He abandoned the So'to to their sad fate, leaving them to face the Fadre and Fañuru alone. Wanadi's farewell is the saddest episode in the entire *Watunna*.

Soon after Wanadi's farewell, the *Watunna* says the Fañuru invaded the Orinoco region from Caracas, seizing the city of Angostura where the So'to's friend, Iaranavi, was living. Then the armed demons continued their advance up the Caura River and entered Makiritare territory. This final campaign took place in 1775 when Governor Centu-rión sent a force out from Angostura under the command of Captain Barreto and Lieutenant Santos de la Puente to invade the Erebato, Vo-tamo, and Padamo Rivers. They were attempting to secure a perma-nent route between Angostura and La Esmeralda. Overrunning the So'to, they established nineteen small forts along their way.

Legend says that a Makiritare shaman named Mahaiwadi led the resistance and repelled the intruders. This character probably corre-sponds to a real one as there are many instances during the Conquest in which native shamans took on the leadership in the war against the Spaniards. What does not correspond to historical reality is the sup-posed taking of Angostura by the Spanish in that same epoch. This event actually took place in 1817, or forty-two years after Mahaiwadi's victory over the Fañuru, and represents one of Simón Bolivar's most celebrated offensives in the Venezuelan War of Independence. This is a perfectly natural chronological error in the world of the legends. As for the fantastic version of Iaranavi's defeat in 1775 at the hands of the Fañuru from Caracas, there is only one likely explanation for its ori-gins.

As has been said, in its early years, Angostura's relations with the So'to had been very good. Only after the forced proselytism at La Es-meralda by Father Jerez did the situation radically change. The Capu-chin also had bad relations with Centurión, the anticlerical command-er of Angostura, but his mission among the Makiritare received the support of Solano, the commander-in-chief in Caracas. It is probable that Jerez told the So'to that his mission depended exclusively on Ca-racas and no longer on Angostura. This fact could explain the Indians' interpretation that the Fadre were friends of Fañuru in Caracas and thus enemies of Iaranavi, the white man from Angostura.

Because of Mahaiwadi's victory over the invaders, the So'to no doubt felt anxious over possible Spanish reprisals against their lands, reprisals which never came. The Spanish gave up their dream of con-quering the Upper Orinoco forever. Nevertheless, the story of the exodus of a part of the tribe from Ihuruña to the East under the com-mand of a dynasty of Makiritare chiefs named the Waitie, seems to correspond to this time. Groups of Makiritare emigrated to the Urari-coera and Mt. Roraima where the Ët'i (Makushi and Taulipang) lived and still live today. These emigrants observed the Ët'i's dealings with the Caribs and Dutch from the Essequibo River. Deprived of all access to Angostura and the Spaniard's coveted goods, they discovered the way to Dutch Guyana and established a friendship with distant Amenadiña, the commercial capital of those rich foreigners whom legend describes as 'people of Wanadi', which is to say, good people, friends of the So'to, just as Iaranavi had once been.

THE WATUNNA

The myths of the Makiritare are the story of what the 'Old People', the Heavenly Ancestors, did. These deeds serve as models for the So'to's behavior. They are the perfect expression of tribal law, the wisdom bequeathed to the Earth by the Primordial Beings. This tradition, which the Makiritare call *Watunna*, has been handed down from generation to generation since the beginning of time in a series of magico-religious festivals known as *Wanwanna*. These rituals, which include dancing, singing, drinking, and a trancelike communion leading to a total collective frenzy, are used to inaugurate the new gardens and communal houses.

The New Conuco or Garden Festival, *Adahe ademi hidi,* begins with great activity in the village. The women pull out the yuca presses and begin preparing cassava bread and other foods. A great canoe, painted with ritual drawings, is used like a bowl to ferment the *iarake* drink whose quantity will determine the ecstasy and length (usually three to five days and nights) of the festival. Now from a path in the jungle leading from the new garden to the village, the men approach, blowing as hard as they can on horns made from *wamehiye* bark. The deep mooing sound of the horns is identified with that of the jungle spirits and calls the supernatural beings to the village to participate in the *Wanwanna*. The musicians enter into the *hododo,* the cleared circular area surrounding the roundhouse. They are loaded down with *wasai* palm, bamboo, bird feathers and seed pods. With these materials they start work on the ceremonial skirts and crowns they will wear during the *Wanwanna*. They also begin making necklaces, earrings, bracelets, staffs hung with multi-colored birds and the long *wanna* bamboo flutes. They begin painting their bodies with magic designs taken from the myths themselves. Now the drinking starts and the excitement picks up. A group of adolescents, invited to participate in the festival for the first time, joins the men to help in the preparations. Some men begin the traditional wrestling. On their shoulders are wooden triangles from which electric eels hang, communicating strength and bravery. The eel is the master of Akuena, the Celestial Lake, and the guardian of the electric ray and manly strength.

Once the preparations have ended, an elder leads a procession of the boys who will sing and dance for the first time. This is the master of the *Wanwanna* dance. He picks up the insignia of his office, the *wasaha*, the rhythm staff from which deer hooves are hung like rattles.

Now the ceremonial fire is lit in the center of the dance floor near which is seated an old man, the Master of Song. The debutantes begin the dance around this center, forming a circular chain, left hand on the shoulder of the person in front. In the other hand is a *wanna*, the bamboo clarinet from which come endless, low, monotonous cries. They listen to the master's voice, that of the wisest elder, the Ademi edamo, the Master of Song, who sings the law of the people in the form of myths. Only the elders completely know the secrets of the *ademi*, whose meanings they have discovered, little by little, over a lifetime of participation in the repeated *Wanwanna*. They have made contact with the *sadashe*, the animal masters and grandfather spirits. They have gained the wisdom and power which the *Watunna* has opened to them. That's why the people call these old men Watunei — 'the ones who know the tradition'.

The Watunei enjoy a privileged position with universal respect. The young person never dares to sit next to them while eating, and remains silent in their presence. These young people cannot understand the *ademi*, the secret meaning of which is not revealed by explanations. Those who know it say that the language of the *sadashe* cannot be translated to ordinary people. The *Adahe ademi hidi*, the ritual complex of the tribe's great myths, must be comprehended directly, like dreaming. It is an intuitive communication increasing in accordance with the initiate's progressive mental change. It is only through submission to the rigorous demands of the initiation that the candidate can receive it. It is only through patience and passiveness.

The techniques for opening consciousness through song and myth are simple and well known to the So'to. They are determined by various rules which the ancestral spirits taught to Wahnatu, the first man on the Earth. The exclusive purpose of the initiatic technique is the rupture of the ordinary mental state in order to achieve a direct, nonrational communication with the supernatural world. The mind hoping to achieve this will have to turn itself into a free, spontaneous force. That's why these teachings can't be communicated in everyday language. There is no professor of 'Heavenly Language'. The student cannot learn this language the way he learns that of another earthly tribe. He has to do it through his own strength, developing his own new powers of hearing.

The traditional method of initiation is to completely wear out and weaken the body's normal instinctive resistance to achieve contact with the world of the *sadashe*. This requires that the candidate go through an intensive preliminary fast accompanied by isolation and silence. This initiatic period marks the end of his childhood, during which he has lived with the women. Now the adult males will submit him to tests of strength and resistance to pain; tests which include the application of poisonous biting ants whose magic effects consist in imparting courage, strength, and skill in his future male duties such as hunting, fighting, cutting trees, clearing gardens, and making houses.

A little before the ritual seclusion, the adolescent will have received practical training in these new duties, accompanying his elders in their work and forays in the forest. If, in the course of this period of practical instruction, the boy has shown satisfactory signs of obedience, discipline, a noncompetitive community spirit, and physical aptitude, he will suddenly be separated from his mother, grandmother, and other women of his extended family who have been responsible for his childhood education. Now he is submitted to the strict period of fasting and seclusion which will prepare him for the spiritual entrance into the cooperative circle of his sex. Finally, he is brought into the ritual gathering of the *Wanwanna* for his first participation in the religious secrets of the tribe. He begins several sleepless days and nights of continuous drinking, dancing, and singing, the monotony and power of which will succeed in breaking down the normal functions of both body and mind.

The youth is immediately forced to drink huge quantities of *iarake*. When he finally collapses from drunkenness, the Master of Dance rejoices, screaming the ritual word 'Neumai', 'he's dead', which means that the candidate has entered into another state of consciousness, similar to that of death. At no moment can the youth allow himself to fall asleep. His companions lift him up and force him to move about and vomit so as to expel the impurities or evil spirits hidden in his body. He must force himself in this strange waking dream to go on drinking more and more *iarake* while periodically vomiting to make room for still more. He must go on dancing and singing and listening, never for a moment losing contact with the spinning world around him. That's the way one learns how to conquer death—entering the collective trance of the dancers, singing, listening, responding, lost in the monotony of movement and song, integrating further and further into the telepathic circle of So'to in the communion of ritual.

Listening to the words of the Master, the dancers' task is to immediately and accurately repeat them. The Ademi edamo, however, sings in such a way as to make the comprehension of his words as difficult as possible. He wants to sharpen the senses of the youths, musicians, and dancers to their absolute maximum. As if absorbed in himself, he sings in a very low, almost inarticulate voice. In order to hear the words, the initiates bring the noise of their steps and the sound of their instruments down to a bare minimum, drawing close enough to the Master to see the fleeting whisper itself escape from his lips. And so they get it and repeat it, just the way the hunter gets and repeats the song of the bird he draws near in order to kill. They open their eyes and ears. They hold their breath. They wait for the words and pry into the mind of the Master. The students' mental concentration now is extraordinary, the repetition unerring, even though in the beginning the sounds were unintelligible.

The sacred songs sung in the *Wanwanna* are in a strange language very different from the everyday speech of the Makiritare. These ritual orations called *ademi* or *aichudi,* belong to the language of the *sadashe,* the primordial spirits and masters of the tribes. The *ademi* were given for everyone at the beginning of time and cannot be altered in any way by men. Nevertheless, their semantic uniqueness does show signs of certain simple tricks of human origin: archaic words, others taken from neighboring tribes, more or less phonetically deformed, complicated ritual endings concealing words from normal daily usage, refrains with no definite meaning, inarticulate vocables, onomatopoeias, whistles, jungle and water sounds, animal movements. As the initiate begins to understand this language, he immediately grasps its phonetic essence, its music, without paying any attention to the meaning of the individual words. Those who still don't understand it, perceive no more than incoherent madness.

On the final night of the *Wanwanna,* after several consecutive days of intoxication, the music suddenly stops. Now the Ademi edamo stands near the central fire and begins the closing of the festival with the solemn singing of the *Adahe ademi hidi* pertaining to the *Watunna*'s principal creation myths. Without accompaniment of drum or horn, the dancers continue their rhythm, approaching and retreating from the center where the fire and the Master are located. Like the other participants, they listen with great silence to the true, unaltered text of the *Watunna*.

The most important *ademi* go on for the entire night without interruption. By dawn, it's just an unintelligible murmur. The participants are like automatons moved by an invisible force. They remove their ritual costumes, their palm skirts, the feathered crowns and fetishes, and toss them into the fire. This is the sign of farewell to the spirits, preparing the men for their return to earth. From these remains, the last flames burst from the fire and the Ademi edamo goes on whispering until they have turned to coals. Now the dancers draw near and enter the fire, stamping the embers with their bare feet. They cannot be burned. It is the final test in their initiation, the authentication of their trance, a display of their new magic powers obtained from the *sadashe*. Like the mythic twins, Iureke and Shikiemona, the initiates have become masters of fire, true men, disciples of *Wanwanna*. Moments later, they leave the roundhouse and collapse on the ground, completely exhausted from their superhuman ordeal.

The *Watunna* is in its essence a secret teaching restricted to the circle of men who undergo the initiations of the *Wanwanna* festivals.* But there is another, popular *Watunna* which belongs to everyone regardless of sex or age, and this is the *Watunna* which is told daily outside the ritual dance circle. It is an exoteric *Watunna* told in everyday language, a profane reflection of that of the sacred space.

These popular versions which form an integral part of every Makiritare's daily life and recreation differ in fundamental ways from the *ademi* heard in the *Wanwanna*. The *ademi* are rigid and exact texts

---

*There is a separate initiation for young women which also includes *ademi* and is performed for the individual girl immediately upon her first menstruation. This initial ceremony, the Ahishto Hya'cadi, in which her head is completely shaved, is followed approximately three months later by the Yena Cajodi, or First Iarake Ceremony, wherein her newly grown hair is cut in the women's style and she is introduced to the whole tribe as an adult, now ready for marriage. In addition to this, it should be mentioned that there is an exclusively female portion of the *Adahe ademi hidi*, taking place several months after the initial *Wanwanna* just before the rains at the end of March. This ceremony, called the *Awanso catajo*, celebrates the first yuca planted in the new garden and insures its success.

which cannot be altered in any way without losing their oral power. They are the *Watunna* exactly as the *sadashe* revealed it to the So'to, and to change them in any way whatsoever would be to rob the *Wanwanna* not only of its initiatic effectiveness, but also of its ability to communicate with the spirit world and thus influence it. But once outside the *Wanwanna,* everyone, including the women and children, is free to tell the stories in whatever form they like. These variations, altered and abbreviated, subject to personal interpretations and the teller's level of knowledge and memory, still fulfill the *Watunna*'s essential role of teaching the tribe's history and spreading its ethical and social ideals. More concerned with the anecdotal aspects of the *ademi* however, these popular versions are unable to preserve the symbolic structure created by their secret language. The phonetic games and mental associations which are such an important part of the sacred dance cannot be translated into profane language.

Sacred or profane, the *Watunna* is a living tradition in constant use. It is hard to pass a day among the Makiritare without hearing a tale or at least some isolated fragment of a story as it relates to the circumstance at hand. You may be hunting or travelling, fishing or basketmaking, there will always be a *Watunna* tale to give some insight into the event. Perhaps it will just be an allusion to a hero or an episode. Perhaps it will be late at night and you'll be lying in your hammock and there'll be time for much more than that. Whatever the situation, there will be a story about something that happened a long time ago.

WANADI

SERUHE IANADI

There was Kahuña, the Sky Place. The Kahuhana lived there, just like now. They're good, wise people. And they were in the beginning too. They never died. There was no sickness, no evil, no war. The whole world was Sky. No one worked. No one looked for food. Food was always there, ready.

There were no animals, no demons, no clouds, no winds. There was just light. In the highest Sky was Wanadi, just like now. He gave his light to the people, to the Kahuhana. He lit everything down to the very bottom, down to Nono, the Earth. Because of that light, the people were always happy. They had life. They couldn't die. There was no separation between Sky and Earth. Sky had no door like it does now. There was no night, like now. Wanadi is like a sun that never sets. It was always day. The Earth was like a part of the Sky.

The Kahuhana had many houses and villages in Kahuña and they were all filled with light. No one lived on the Earth. There was no one there, nothing, just the Earth and nothing else.

Wanadi said: "I want to make people down there." He sent his messenger, a *damodede*. He was born here to make houses and good people, like in the Sky Place. That *damodede* was Wanadi's spirit. He was the Earth's first Wanadi, made by the other Wanadi who lives in Kahuña. That other Wanadi never came down to the Earth. The one that came was the other's spirit.

Later on, two more *damodede* came here. They were other forms of Wanadi's spirit.

The first Wanadi to come was called Seruhe Ianadi, the Wise. When he came, he brought knowledge, tobacco, the maraca, and the *wiriki*. He smoked and he sang and he made the old people. That was a long time before us, the people of today.

When that spirit was born, he cut his navel-cord and buried the placenta. He didn't know. Now the worms got into the placenta and they started to eat it. The placenta rotted. As it rotted, it gave birth to a man, a human creature, ugly and evil and all covered with hair like an animal. It was Kahu. He has different names. They call him Kahushawa and Odosha too. This man was very evil. He was jealous of Wanadi. He wanted to be master of the Earth. Because of him, we suffer now. There's hunger, sickness and war. He's the father of all the Odoshankomo. Now, because of him, we die.

When that old Wanadi's placenta rotted, Odosha sprang out of the Earth like a spear. He said: "This Earth is mine. Now there's going to be war. I'm going to chase Wanadi out of here."

He misled those people who had just been born. He taught them to kill. There was a man fishing. He had lots of fish. Odosha told them: "If you kill him, you'll have lots of fish."

They killed him. Odosha was happy. Then the people were turned into animals as punishment.

Because of Odosha, Seruhe Ianadi couldn't do anything on Earth. He went back to the Sky and left the old people as animals with Odosha. He didn't leave any of Wanadi's people on the Earth though. That was the end of the first people.

The birth of Kahu on that old Earth is a sign to us, the people of today. When a baby is born, we should never bury the placenta. The worms get it. It rots. Another Odosha will come again, like in the beginning to hurt the baby, to kill it. Like what happened when Kahu fought against Wanadi for control of the Earth. When a baby is born, we put the placenta in a nest of white ants. It's safe there. The worms can't get it. Okay. Now you can bury the nest of white ants.

That was the story of the old people. That's all.

NADEIUMADI

Later on, the other Wanadi, the one that never left Kahuña, thought: "I want to know what's happening on Earth. I want good people living down there."

So he sent a second Wanadi, a *damodede* called Nadeiumadi. When he came there, he thought: "The people are going to die now because Odosha is here. Because of Odosha they're sick. They're dying. But I'm here now. People are going to be born again soon. Through my power, they're going to live again. Death isn't real. It's one of Odosha's tricks. People are going to live now."

The new Wanadi wanted to give a sign, a show of his power. He did it to show us that death isn't real. He sat down. He put his elbows on his knees, his head in his hands. He just sat there in silence, thinking, dreaming, dreaming. He dreamt that a woman was born. It was his mother. She was called Kumariawa. That's the way it happened. That man was thinking and smoking. He was quietly blowing tobacco, dreaming of his mother, Kumariawa. That's the way she was born. He made his own mother. That's the way they tell it. He gave birth to her dreaming, with tobacco smoke, with the song of his maraca, singing and nothing else.

Now Kumariawa stood up and Wanadi thought: "You're going to die." So Wanadi dreamed that he killed his mother. She was born full-grown, big like a woman. She wasn't born like a baby. And right away she died, when he dreamed her death, playing the maraca and singing. It wasn't Odosha who killed her but him himself. He had a lot of power when he thought. When he thought: "Life." Then Kumariawa was born. When he thought: "Death." Then she died. Wanadi made her as a sign of his power, of his wisdom. He knew that that wasn't real. Death was a trick.

The new Wanadi had *Huehanna*. He brought it from Kahuña to make people with. He wanted new people for the Earth. He wanted lots of people. *Huehanna* was like a great ball, huge and hollow, with a thick, heavy shell as hard as stone. It was called *Huehanna*. Inside *Huehanna* you could hear noises, words, songs, laughter, screaming. It was filled with people. You couldn't see them. You could just hear them. Wanadi's unborn people were all in there talking. He brought them down to Earth from Heaven. They were happy. That's why they were singing and dancing and making so much noise before being born. Wanadi wanted *Huehanna* opened on the Earth so its people could spread over it. "They'll die," he thought, "because Odosha is here. He doesn't want them to live. He doesn't want good people. He's going to make them sick. He's going to kill them as soon as they come out. But I'll bring them back to life. They'll get born again and won't die."

Wanadi killed Kumariawa as an example. He did it to bring her back to life again. He wanted to show Odosha his power. He was the master of life. His people can't die. Now when he killed his mother, he thought: "She's dead. She'll come back again soon. She'll live again just as my people will live again. Because Odosha's going to kill them as soon as they come out of *Huehanna*. But I'll make them live again."

After he killed Kumariawa, he went hunting. When he left, he said: "I'm going." He called Kudewa and asked him to help bury the woman. It was the first burial. They buried Kumariawa in the ground. "I'm going," he told Kudewa. "I'm going hunting. I'll be back soon. Guard the grave. Kumariawa is going to reappear in this spot. When she comes out, it will be a signal for the people to come out of *Huehanna* and live. Watch my mother's body. Don't let Odosha near it." Now he called his nephew, Iarakaru. "Watch *Huehanna!*" he called out as he left.

Wanadi forgot his *chakara*. That's where he kept his power, his tobacco, his cigarettes. He kept the night in the *chakara* too, because at that time, they didn't know about the night. There was only light on the Earth like in the Heavens. It was all one world, Sky above and daylight here below. When Wanadi got tired, he just opened the *chakara* and stuck his head inside and slept. Hidden sleep, the night, was in there. That's the way he slept. When he got up he closed the *chakara* again and shut the night inside.

Wanadi had warned Iarakuru: "Never play with the *chakara*. It's my power! Be careful! Don't open it. If you do, the night will get out."

When Wanadi left, Kudewa kept guard over Kumariawa. Kudewa kept watching to let out a scream when it began to move, when the body began to rise again. "Call me right away. Shout and I'll come," Wanadi told him when he left.

When the ground began to move, Wanadi was far away. Kudewa saw a hand stick out, Kumariawa's arm. The earth opened. He turned into a parrot and began to shout and scream the warning. When Wanadi heard him, he came running to see what his new mother looked like. He came running to see if the *Huehanna* had burst. As he ran, night fell. All at once, EVERYTHING went dark. Suddenly, the WHOLE world went out and Wanadi was running through the night. "They opened the *chakara*," he thought. "Iarakaru did it." And that's just what happened. Iarakaru was too curious. Someone said to him: "Open it!" It was Odosha. He didn't see him. He just heard him, like in a dream. "Open it!" Odosha said. "You'll learn the secret." It was as if Iarakaru was dreaming. At first he didn't dare. And then he did it. "What's this secret hidden in Wanadi's *chakara*?" he thought. "I want to see. I want to smoke and be powerful like Wanadi. I want to meet the night." So he opened the *chakara* to look inside and right away the night burst out. Sky hid itself. The light went out over the Earth.

That's the way darkness came to our world. It was Iarakaru's fault. It didn't exist before that. I didn't see it. But that's the way it's told.

When it burst, he was like a blind man. He couldn't see Sky or Earth. He was terrified. He just started running in the dark, not like a man but like a white monkey. And that's the way he stayed, as punishment. He's the grandfather of all the iarakaru (capuchin monkeys) that exist today. He was the first one. He gave them their form. As soon as they were born, the monkeys took his form. That's why they call them iarakaru. They're all children of that same Iarakaru, the one who let out the night long ago. He was Wanadi's nephew and he was punished. That's the way they tell it.

When Wanadi went hunting, Odosha thought: "That man has power. He wants to make his own people on the Earth. He thinks the Earth is his. He thinks he owns everything, that his people are going to be born, that it's always going to be light. He left that woman's body in the ground and he thinks, 'She's dead but she's going to live again. *Huehanna* will open'. He left guards to warn him when the signal comes. I don't like it. The Earth is mine, not his. I'm not going to let

Kumariawa out of her corpse nor the people out of *Huehanna*."

Then Odosha hid. He spoke to Iarakaru as in a dream. He said: "Open the *chakara*!"

He was happy when it was opened. "Now it's dark. The night is mine. No one's going to live. I'm the ruler of the Earth."

He had his own people. They could see and move and do lots of things in the dark. Wanadi's people couldn't see. They couldn't do a thing, just be scared and nothing else. This really made Odosha happy.

Odosha sent a hairy dwarf named Ududi to watch the grave. Ududi told him: "She's coming out!" Odosha heard him and knew what to do. He pissed in a gourd. He gave it to Makako and sent him to the woman's grave. Makako was like a small lizard. He ran with the gourd full of urine. Kumariawa split the Earth and began to rise. The little lizard threw the gourd. Odosha's urine was like a poison, seething with fire. It covered the woman. It scorched her body. The flesh was roasted. The bones fell apart. The parrot kept on screaming and the Earth closed up. "It's done," said Makako when he went back to Odosha.

When Wanadi arrived, he found darkness, ashes, bones, cinders, the monkey gone, the parrot silent, the *chakara* opened. "I can't do anything now," he thought. "There's no flesh, no body. She won't come back to life. There's no light. The Earth isn't mine anymore. The people will all die now."

Then he went to find *Huehanna*. It was still there. Those people were inside there, screaming, shaking with fear. They hadn't been born. They hadn't died. They weren't anything yet, like in the beginning. They couldn't be born. When he burned the woman, Odosha went with Makako to open *Huehanna*, to smash it to pieces, to kill the people about to come out. They found it and started beating it with their clubs, but nothing happened. They couldn't do a thing to it. *Huehanna* was as hard as a stone with that thick shell. They couldn't break it. They just left it there.

Wanadi found *Huehanna*. When he picked it up, he heard the voices inside. It made him sad. "They'll have to wait now," he thought. "I'm going to hide them." He took them to Mount Waruma hidi. He hid *Huehanna* with all the unborn people up in that mountain.

It's waiting there, in peace, since the beginning of the world, and it will stay there till the end. When the night came, Wanadi hid *Huehanna*. The good people inside haven't been born yet. They haven't died either. They're waiting there in Waruma hidi for the end of the world, for the death of Odosha.

Odosha is the ruler of our world, but he's not eternal. He'll die when evil disappears. Then Wanadi will go back to Waruma hidi again. The light from Kahuña will shine once more. We'll see Heaven from here like in the beginning. Wanadi will come looking for *Huehanna*. The good, wise people who couldn't be born in the beginning will finally be born. He'll tell his people that the time has come. In the place called Warumaña, they're waiting. I haven't seen it. But that's what it's called.

Wanadi left the Earth in darkness. He left it to Odosha and went back to Heaven. He put Kumariawa's skull and bones in a palm basket and took them with him. He threw his mother's bones into Lake Aku-ena and the woman came back to life once again. She's still living there in Heaven now.

I haven't seen her. But that's what they say.

ATTAWANADI

When that man came, there was no light.
The old people were living in fear, hiding like animals. They couldn't
move. They couldn't see anything. They had to look for food and water, but they couldn't that way. They were living with Odosha, in misery, in hunger. Odosha frightened them. He made them sick. He killed
them. The other Wanadi blew on a *wiriki*. And so Attawanadi was
born.

That man was a new Wanadi. He was the third *damodede* of the
other Wanadi who shines in the highest Heaven. He was sent down
from Kahuña to see what was happening on Earth, to make people
again, good people, Wanadi people. He made Shi, the sun, Nuna, the
moon, and Shiriche, the stars. They were like people and lit up this
Earth's new Sky. The real Sky couldn't be seen anymore. Because of
Odosha, the light up there, the light from the other Wanadi, didn't
come down anymore. That's why the new Wanadi made this sun for
us, to make it light for us during the day. When the new Wanadi came,
it dawned again. The old people were happy. One by one they came
out of their caves to look at Shi, the new sun, the new day. Then they
knew that Wanadi had returned. Now the Earth has its own sun. You
could see a sky above the Earth again, the Earth's own sky. You
couldn't see Kahuña, the real Sky anymore, like in the beginning, nor
the Kahuhana, the ones who live in the Sky. Now the Earth has its
own sky. "It's done," that man said. "Now the Earth has its sun, its
moon, its light." Then the old people rejoiced.

Now those old people gathered around the new Wanadi. They com-
plained about Odosha. "There's hunger," they said. "Misery, sickness,
death." They were like animals. They had animal bodies. When they
wanted to, they took their human ones again. They didn't have any-

thing: no cassava, no water, no clothes, no houses, no arrows, no bows, no hammocks. Nothing, just misery and fear, like animals.

Wanadi saw Iarakaru, the monkey. He was skinny now. He was complaining too. "It's your fault," said Wanadi. "This suffering's all because of you. You're thin as punishment. You're going to stay that way, your children and grandchildren too."

Now that man thought: "I'll make the Earth good again. I'll remake everything, like in the beginning."

"I'm going," he said. "I'll be back soon." Now he went to Kahuña, to Iamankave, the food mistress's house. He asked for food for the Earth. "Fine," said Iamankave. And she sent a messenger down to Earth with lots of cassava. Now they ate. They danced when that man from Kahuña came with the cassava.

Then Odosha came. He was furious. "Wanadi's back," he said. "He wants to be master of the Earth again."

There were two children, a boy and a girl. When Wanadi went to Heaven to look for food, Odosha dressed up like Wanadi and went to trick them. "I'm Wanadi," he said. "Now I'm going to teach you how to fuck." And he showed them. That's why they did it. Before that, they didn't know how. The old people never used to do that. When they started, they got sick. They got punished. The Kahuhana with the cassava didn't come back again. There wasn't any more food now. A lot of them died.

Then Wanadi returned. "Okay," he said. "What am I going to do now? These people are no good now. They can only hear Odosha. They don't want to be Wanadi's people anymore. I'll make new people, real people."

He built a house on Wana hidi, a mountain on the Kuntinama. It was the first house. That spirit made it for himself, as a sign for the people. Then he made another, and another and another, for the people. He showed them how to make their houses, not like animals anymore, but like people. He made lots of houses. He made villages. That's why they call him Attawanadi, House-Wanadi.

When Wanadi made his house on Wana hidi, Odosha came and saw it. He made another one just like it right in front of it. "Okay," said Wanadi. "I've got to do everything fast before Odosha spoils it."

Wanadi set down some people next to him in Wana hidi. They were twelve men called *Wanadi sottoi*, Wanadi's people. They were very strong and wise. Odosha had lots of people of his own in his house too, the Odoshankomo. They were evil. They wanted to destroy Wanadi.

Wanadi sat down, silent, calm, not eating, not doing anything. He put his elbows on his knees, his head in his hands. He was just thinking, dreaming. Dreaming. That's the way Wanadi did everything. "This is what I dream," he would say. "I'm dreaming there's lots of food."

No food came. Odosha was right in front of him. He didn't want that. He started dreaming evil. He answered Wanadi with evil.

"I dreamed: we have cassava," said Wanadi, dreaming.

"This is my dream," answered Odosha. "Lots of hunger." He was answering with evil.

"I dreamed this: I killed five deer," said Wanadi, dreaming.

Now the other one answered: "No. I dreamed before you. I dreamed: there's nothing to eat. Many people are dying." He answered with evil.

"I'm dreaming: there are *conucos*. There's yuca everywhere. I'm cutting down the yuca. There's a great harvest."

"Here's how I dreamed first," answered Odosha. "Many sick people. They're all going to die."

Wanadi couldn't do anything because of Odosha. He became angry. "We're leaving," he told the people. "We can't stay here with Odosha. We'll live somewhere else."

"Good," they said. And they left.

They went to Truma achaka. Wade lived there in a cave. "We're fleeing from Odosha," they told him. "That's why we came."

"Okay," said Wade. "You can stay here."

They stayed. Wade was good. He was the grandfather of all the sloths. Whenever he wanted to, he'd take his sloth form. When he left the Earth later on, he left his form here, for the sloths of today.

Wanadi built Wade a house in Truma achaka and left his people there. He went off to make other houses, to make more people for the Earth. "I'm going," he said. "I'll be back soon."

He took his blowgun to hunt along the way. As he was walking, he met a jaguar. He ran ahead and made a platform. The jaguar came up behind him. It wanted to eat him. Now he killed the jaguar with this blowgun. Now the jaguar got up again. It was a spirit jaguar. It couldn't die. Wanadi left. Then he dreamed he was killing birds. He really did kill birds. He brought them back to Wade's house.

"I'm back," he said. "I brought you food." They were happy. They ate the birds.

"A jaguar jumped out along the way," said Wanadi. "It wanted to eat me. I killed it with my blowgun. It fled."

"Sure it wasn't one of Odosha's tricks? It wasn't Odosha as a jaguar that you met?" said Wade. "Next time when you go out, don't go as Wanadi."

"Okay," said Wanadi. Next time he went out as a hunter, all old and dirty, not like Wanadi.

Now he met Odosha as the real Odosha. Odosha stared at him. He didn't know who he was. "You haven't seen Wanadi, have you?" he asked.

"Who's Wanadi?" he answered. "I don't know him."

"The one who used to live in Wana hidi," said Odosha. "He ran away. I'm trying to find him. You haven't seen him, have you?"

"Who's Wanadi?" Wanadi answered. And so he fooled Odosha. Odosha went the other way, looking and looking. He didn't come back again.

Wanadi went back to his house in Truma achaka. He dreamed more birds. He came back with more birds. His people were happy when he came back. The twelve men ate again.

"I met Odosha on the way," said Wanadi. "He was asking about Wanadi. 'Never heard of him,' I said. He's far away by now, looking, looking."

"Good," said Wade. "That's very good. Now, from now on, don't go out as Wanadi."

Wanadi changed himself and went out again. He went as a hunter, old and dirty. He walked all over, smoking, playing his maraca, making houses, making new people.

Odosha was still lost, still fooled. One day he came to ask at Wade's house. "No. He's not here," they said. "We don't know him." He went off looking again. He couldn't find Wanadi. He didn't know where to look.

Now Attawanadi made lots of houses and good people.

KAWESHAWA

Wanadi was living at Wade's house. At daybreak he went out to fish in the Kunukunuma. He came to Tukudi Rapids and threw his hook and *kurahua* line in the water. He caught some creature that lived in the water. Inside the water, she had a fish body. Outside the water, she was a beautiful woman. Wanadi didn't see her as a fish, but as a woman. "I like her," he thought. "I'm going to marry her." Then he set her loose.

"You didn't ask permission," the woman said. "You can't fish here without my permission."

"What's your name? Where do you live?"

"My name is Kaweshawa. My father's the fish master. I live in the river, in Kasuruña Rapids. My father's village is deep below."

Wanadi tries to grab her. She slips through his fingers. She hides in the water. A little ways down, she pops out again.

"Come out of the river," Wanadi calls. "Come home with me."

Kaweshawa yells: "Come out of the land. Follow me home to my father's."

But Wanadi doesn't want to.

"I'll catch you!" he says. And he throws his hook in the river. Kaweshawa comes up, takes a bite and gets caught. Wanadi gives a jerk. Kaweshawa gets loose. Wanadi goes flying back over the rocks. "I've got a better hook," he says. He picks up a beautiful necklace and throws it in. She looks at the necklace, grabs it and starts to pull. He stands up on the shore, gets a good grip and plants his feet. His heels leave marks in the rocks. They haven't washed away. You can still see them there on the shore at Tukudi. Now the woman pulls and pulls and the man lets go of the necklace. Rolling with laughter, she puts it around her neck.

32

"Okay. You win," says Wanadi. "I'll catch you this time."

She plays with him. She comes up to the shore and shows off her necklace, raising her body out of the water. Wanadi sticks out an *amoahocho*. The woman sticks her finger in and yanks on it. Wanadi lets go and falls down, sprawling over the rocks. Kaweshawa lets out a laugh.

"Give me the *amoahocho* again, to see if you can catch me."

"Okay, we'll try it again. This time I won't fall." That man walks over, stands up straight and leans his back against a rock. The woman sticks her finger in the *amoahocho* and pulls with all her might. Wanadi has a good grip. He doesn't let go. Kaweshawa pulls and pulls toward the river. Wanadi pulls toward the earth to see who'll win. Kaweshawa wins and Wanadi falls in the water.

"Let's go to my father's house," says Kaweshawa.

They say that Wanadi played that way with Kaweshawa to give us a sign. And so during the dances and festivals, that's the way we play with women. We try to catch them with *amoahocho*. Everyone watches to see who wins. If we win, we take the woman.

Wanadi fell in the Kunukunuma with a great splash, an enormous whirl of arms and legs. They fought together in the water as the current carried them off.

"Let me go!" screamed Wanadi. "I'm no fish. I can't breathe in here!" He looked at Kaweshawa again. He saw her as a fish because he was in the river now.

"Don't be afraid. Now you'll see my village with the eyes of a fish." She blew some herbs over Wanadi. He stopped seeing the water the way people see it. He could breathe now. He saw all the fish and *mawadi* on the bottom of the river with their houses and *conucos*.

"Now you can follow me. We're going to my father's house. You're my husband now. That's why I blew on you." Kaweshawa dragged him along. He was her prisoner. He didn't want to live under the water.

Crashing and swirling, they were pulled downstream. For three days they went down like that. Wanadi wanted to get back on land and take the woman to his house. When they got to Kasuruña Rapids, they were tired. Wanadi dragged Kaweshawa up by her hair onto a flat rock by the shore. They sat there recovering. They cured each other with the evil eye.

When they heard he wanted to get married, people began coming to give Wanadi advice. First his nephew Iarakaru came and said: "Don't go sleeping with that woman. I know her. She breeds piranha. She has them hidden in her vagina. They protect it. They bit Opossum. When he tried to sleep with that woman, they took it right off. I tried too and they cut mine off as well."

Wanadi didn't pay any attention. Now Esheu, the coati, and Odoma, the paca, came by. "If you want to marry that woman," they told Wanadi, "we'll help you. We'll kill the keepers of her vagina."

"Okay," said Wanadi. "I'll wait and you clear the way for me."

Wanadi left Kaweshawa with his friends and went off to sleep alone.

Esheu got an iron needle from Ahisha, the egret. He stuck it in his penis and went off with Kaweshawa. The piranha bit into it. Their teeth all cracked and fell out. Coati deflowered that woman. Then Odoma did the same thing. They tricked Kaweshawa. They weren't castrated.

They went to tell Wanadi. "There's no more danger. We've cleared the way. Nothing happened to us. Now you can try it too." And they gave him the iron needle.

"I don't like this iron thing," said Wanadi. "I'll try something else. I'll kill the piranha with *ayadi* (barbasco). That'll get them out of their hole."

He got an *ayadi* vine and began to beat it on a rock. White juice flowed out. Wanadi took Kaweshawa by the hair. He stuck the barbasco in her vagina. That was the first *T'denke,* the first time they fished with barbasco.

The piranha came floating out, asleep. They just scooped them up with their *wahi* nets. They filled their baskets with them. They ate for three days. The piranha were good.

Wanadi was happy. "It's done. You're cured now. Now you're fine. You'll be my wife."

He went down in the river with her, into Kasuruña Rapids, down to his father-in-law, the fish master's house.

"Here. I've brought your son-in-law," said the woman.

"Good," said her father.

"Here I am," said Wanadi. "You're my father-in-law. I'm going to work for you. I'm going to pay you. I'm going to pay for my wife. We'll move to the land. When I finish the new house, we'll call all the people together to dance and sing."

"You're all right," said the fish master.

"I'm Wanadi. When the house is ready, then I'll sleep with your daughter, then I'll go hunting and fishing and bring back food for you. When my wife has children, I'll make another house. I'll move with my wife and child."

"Good," said the father-in-law. "You're a good man."

Wanadi slept in the house. He didn't touch Kaweshawa. When the sun rose, he went out and started his father-in-law's new house up on a mountain called Kushamakari.

He made it large and beautiful, as a sign, to show men what they should do. Then Wanadi moved with his in-laws and his wife. He began to serve, to work. He went hunting and fishing. When everything was ready, they had a great feast and danced.

Wanadi made another house in secret. He built it on a different mountain which is also called Kushamakari, up behind the Duida, in front of Marahuaka. No one knew about it. Only he did. No one else. He didn't say anything. He'd just go out. No one knew where he was going. He'd say: "I'm going hunting." It was a trick. He was going off to work at the other Kushamakari. They thought he'd really gone hunting. They said: "What's he doing out there all this time?" Much later, after he'd said good by to the Earth, then he told them. Then they knew he'd made the other Kushamakari. It was hidden deep in the mountains. They also found out what the other house was for. But, for now, his in-laws just said: "Wanadi went hunting." They were fooled. He would disappear around sunset. By morning he was back working on the Kushamakari the people could see. "It's the only Kushamakari," the people thought. They couldn't see the other one.

The other Kushamakari is hidden in the headwaters of the Kawai and Iamo, in front of Marahuaka. It's very hard to get there. Lots of rapids for canoes. Lots of *mawadi* living there to guard the way. You have to sing a lot to get there. You can't eat meat or sleep with women either. A huge bat guards the cave. He's always watching there. Only powerful, good beings live there: the blowgun master, the grandfather of the tapirs, and lots of others. Odosha's people never go there. Evil people can't get in. The *mawadi* and the bat eat them if they try.

Okay. Now the sun rose and Wanadi said: "I'm going to look for food. I'm going to kill some curassow."

When he came back, he called his wife. "I killed some curassow. I left them out there on the trail. Go get them."

"Okay," said Kaweshawa. And she went off to get the curassow.

It was a sign. When we come back from hunting, we leave the game on the trail. We don't bring it in the house. The women go out and get it.

When she came to the path, she looked around. She didn't see any curassow. She saw a man standing there.

"I'm Kurunkumo," he said to her. "I'm the curassow. I can't die. Wanadi thinks he killed me and so it appeared. It was a trick."

Then Kurunkumo grabbed Kaweshawa. "I like you," he said. "You're pretty. I'm going to take you home with me."

He turned into a curassow and took off toward Marahuaka, taking Kaweshawa with him. His house is over there. It's called Fauhi ewiti, Curassow Peak.

The next day Wanadi went around to all the houses. "Have you seen Kaweshawa?" he asked.

"No. We haven't seen her," they answered.

"Have you heard anything about her?" he asked.

"No. We haven't heard anything," they answered.

He went everywhere. No one had seen her. Wanadi sat down on a rock, elbows on his knees, head in his hands. "What am I going to do now?" he thought.

Mottodona, the bumblebee, came up.

"Don't bother me with your buzzing," said Wanadi. "I lost my woman."

Mottodona was a *huhai*. He knew everything.

"You can make another woman. There's some white clay near here called *madi*," he said and then he went off and hid again.

Wanadi got up and went to find the *madi*. He shaped it into a woman. He sang. He smoked. He blew tobacco. He dreamed: "It's moving." The *madi* clay came to life. Then Wanadi carried off his white *madi* woman.

Now dawn came and the woman got out of her hammock. She got a big pot and went down to the stream but she didn't return. Wanadi waited for her in the hammock till noon.

"It's noon already," he said. "My woman hasn't come back. I'll go see what happened."

He went to the stream. He couldn't find her. He sat down on a log.

Mottodona, the bumblebee, came by again. "That white woman you made was no good."

"Talk straight. I don't know what you mean."

"I said she was no good. She fell apart in the stream. See how white the water is, like barbasco? Well, that's not barbasco. It's *madi* clay. Go find some *mani (peraman)* resin. It won't dissolve. There are *mani* trees nearby here. Make yourself a beautiful black woman."

Wanadi went to find some *mani*. He made the black woman. He blew tobacco. He sang. He dreamed: "She's moving." He brought her to life. Then he took her home.

When the sun came up, the black woman got out of her hammock, took a basket and went out to get yuca. She didn't come back again. Wanadi went to look for her but he couldn't find any tracks.

"I've lost my woman again."

"She melted on the path, in the sun," said Mottodona. "See that black spot on the trail?"

Wanadi was sitting on his jaguar bench, thinking, thinking. He was sad. He had his feather crown, his maraca, his cigar and his tobacco pouch with little frogs painted on it. He set the maraca down on the pouch. Then he dreamed of one of the frogs painted on the tobacco pouch: "Frog, frog, woman, you're alive, you're a woman." That's the way he sang and smoked. And so a woman was born, Wanadi Hiña-mohüdü. She was born as Wanadi's woman. She was that frog painted on the tobacco pouch. As soon as she came to life she began looking around for colored powders and oils to paint herself with. She just painted and painted herself. Now he thought: "She's no good." He said: "Go somewhere else." So the woman went somewhere else, quietly painting herself.

Then he made another one, a bird woman. When this woman was born, she began laughing. She didn't do anything except laugh. When people came, they'd greet her, but she just laughed. "She's no good," said Wanadi. He got rid of her.

"There's no other woman for me but the first one. She's the only good one. Where is she? What am I doing looking for other women? I'll go look for her again." He said that as a sign, an example, so we don't go out looking for other women when we already have one.

As he was thinking, Mottodona came up. "Nnnnnnnn." That's the way he sang. He was flying and spinning all around.

"Don't bother me," said Wanadi and he shoved him.

He came back to pester him again. He shoved him. "Nnnnnnn. Don't push me. I didn't come to give you any more advice. You want to know where Kaweshawa is?" Then he said: "Your wife is at her new husband's house. His name is Kurunkumo." Then the bumblebee left.

Wanadi went running back to Wade's house. "My wife is at Kurunkumo's house. Mottodona told me. What should I do?"

"You can go get her," said Wade. "But not as Wanadi. You'll have to go disguised."

Wade knew a lot. He was very old. He was a *huhai*. He had a sloth body. His teeth, his hair, his head were all like a sloth.

"You know a lot," Wanadi said to him. "What will the disguise be?"

"I'll lend you my head, my teeth, my skin," said the old man. "C'mon, let's switch."

They switched. Now Wanadi looked like a little old man, like Wade. And Wade, like Wanadi.

"Now watch out for my teeth. Don't go eating any palm hearts," he told him. "In the meantime, I'll be eating all the palm hearts I can. You can give me my teeth back after that."

He started walking to Kurunkumo's house on Curassow Peak. As he was walking, an old woman named Wahiataka came by, hunting animals.

"Here I am," she said. "Are you Wade?"

"I'm Wade," Wanadi told her. "What are you doing here?"

"Hunting and fishing," the old woman said. "I've come from my brother-in-law, Kurunkumo's house."

"Why didn't Kurunkumo come?" Wanadi asked.

"His wife Kaweshawa just gave birth. We're going to celebrate in five days. We're going to dance. That's why I came out to find food," said the old woman. She hadn't killed a single animal yet. "You're Wade," she said. "You're wise. You're a *huhai*. Help me."

"Okay," said Wanadi. "We'll go together. Then we'll go to dance and eat. Now let's fish."

He threw barbasco in the water. He sang. He dreamed fish. They caught a lot. He made a barbecue. He roasted the fish. They ate and ate.

"That's enough," he said. "Now let's go hunting."

They caught tapir, deer. They ate a little and stored the rest to take with them. Then they caught paca and birds. The next day too and the day after that as well.

"Let's go now," said Wanadi. "We have enough and it's already five days. Let's go and dance now."

Now the two of them went off with the animals. Near the house, the old woman said: "Wait for me on the trail. I'll go ahead first."

"Okay," said the sloth. He stayed there.

Wahiataka went on ahead. She arrived at the house. "What happened?" they asked her.

"I brought lots of food, lots of game for the feast," she said. "I met Wade along the way. He caught lots of fish and animals. He wants to come and dance."

"Where is he?" asked Kurunkumo.

"Just outside there. He's waiting for me."

"Watch out. Are you sure it's not one of Wanadi's tricks?"

"It's not Wanadi. It's Wade. I saw his skin, his teeth, his head."

"Are you sure? It's not a trick?" they asked again.

"It was Wade. He's the *sadashe's* friend. I saw his teeth."

"Okay," said Kurunkumo. "I'll go out and get him."

The man looked around for a club. When he found the club, he picked it up and took it with him. Then he went out to find Wade, thinking: "If he's tricking us, I'll kill him." He was thinking about Wanadi. Wanadi was waiting when he got there. Kurunkumo stood there staring and looking. He saw his tiny little eyes, half closed with hair all around them and only a few teeth and a sleepy head drooped to one side like a sloth.

Kurunkumo dropped the club. He spoke to the old man: "You're really Wade? You're not Wanadi? You're not lying?"

"That's right," he answered. "I came to dance with you. I brought lots of food."

"I'll show you the way," said the curassow. He brought him in. He fed him.

As he ate, Wanadi looked at Kaweshawa. She was sitting there, old and dirty, all dishevelled and worn out. She had Kurunkumo's children all around her. She had just given birth. "She's gotten really ugly," thought Wanadi. "She's like another woman."

They started dancing when the sun went down. They said to the sloth-faced old man: "They say you know a lot. You're Wade. Do you know how to sing?"

"I know how to sing," the old man answered.

"Good. We'll let you sing." He began to sing. He sang beautifully, beautifully. Everyone was listening. He really knew a lot. As he sang, the sun rose. As everyone was listening and dancing and drinking, the sun rose.

When day broke, Kurunkumo was drunk. "This old Wade is really ugly," he said. "He's got too much hair. We'll cut it." Now he called his wife. "Bring the scissors." Kaweshawa came with the scissors. The others went on dancing and drinking. The old man and the woman were left alone. She began cutting. As she was cutting, the woman stuck her hand in the sloth's mane. She felt a huge tongue hidden inside it. "What's that? That's like Wanadi's tongue. My old husband Wanadi had a tongue just like that. He had a tongue that stuck right through his head. You're not Wanadi?"

The others were dancing, drunk. They weren't listening. The old man said: "Yes. I'm Wanadi. I came to get you with this disguise. This tongue's the only thing that's mine. The skin and the teeth are Wade's. He lent me his head."

When she heard this, the woman started to weep. "You're my husband. You're Wanadi. I want to go back with you. I'm miserable here. I'm suffering, tired, sick. I have so many children, so much work. This Kurunkumo treats me horrible. Take me home again."

Weeping and crying, the woman told him about the curassow Kurunkumo.

Wanadi said: "You were beautiful before. That's why I loved you. Now you're all broken down and ugly, like an old woman. You're my woman, that's why I came to get you. Okay. Let's go. I'll take you away. Then I'll make you better."

The others just went on dancing and drinking and eating. They weren't listening. The woman stopped crying now. She was happy. She rubbed her hand along her husband, Wanadi's tongue inside Wade's mane. The man closed his little eyes. He was happy. "Good. Let's go," he said. "First let's eat."

He turned into a cockroach. He turned her into a cockroach too. And so, like spirits, the two of them climbed up on the big pile of meat. They ate and ate. The people were all drunk, dancing, drinking, eating. A man saw the two cockroaches eating. He swiped them with his hand. They scrambled up the center post of the house. They went flying up it. When they got to the top, Wanadi became a woodpecker and she became a frog.

Wanadi tonoro is the name of the Wanadi bird, the woodpecker. It was Wanadi's spirit. That spirit left its form here for its children.

"We're leaving," he screamed to the people. "I'm Wanadi. She's Kaweshawa."

They stopped dancing. Kurunkumo became furious. He saw Wade's trick. "There they go!" he screamed. "Get your bows and arrows! Let's kill them!"

With his beak, the woodpecker picked up the frog by the leg. Now he took off from the roof of the house. That frog weighed him down. It made him go very slow. He just kept going up and down, up and down, up and down. That's the same way the Wanadi birds, his grandchildren, fly today. You can see them out there. They fly like that in memory of the beginning. That's what they say.

They went after them. Many of them were so drunk they fell over. They couldn't even shoot straight. The bird and the frog came to a *pijiguao* tree. When he got to it, the Wanadi bird grabbed onto the trunk. They came up behind them, yelling and screaming. They just shot their arrows. Then one of them burned the tree. He set it on fire. The fire burned the bird's tail. That's the way it's been ever since. Then he took off again with the frog in his beak, up and down, up and down. He flew up to another tree, a *pendare* (chicle) tree. He pecked at the trunk with his beak. *Pendare* milk gushed out. The Wanadi bird discovered it. He was the first one. He said: "This is the cure. I'll wash and clean you with *pendare* milk to make you better."

There wasn't time. The others came running up. He took off again for another tree called *marima*. He took milk from the *marima* tree. Again he said: "This is the cure. I'm going to make you better." He just said this as a sign. He didn't have time. The others came to kill him.

Now he flew far away with his wife, the frog, hanging from his beak. Up and down, up and down. They came to a talllll, talllll tree called *Faru hidi*. It went all the way up to Heaven. It's still there. We see it as a mountain now (Mount Paru). *Huhai* see it as it really is, as a tree.

When they got there, the bird climbed up on a branch. They turned into a man and woman, like they really were. "We made it," said Wanadi. "They can't come here. This tree's too high. We're in Heaven now. Let's rest."

They rested.

When they looked down, they couldn't see the Earth anymore. They just saw Akuena, blue water and nothing else. They were high above Lake Akuena, happy.

Now Wanadi looked at his woman and became sad. She wasn't any better. She looked old and ugly and sick. "She's no good like this," he thought. "I'll kill her. Then I'll make her again."

He killed her. When he killed her, he built a barbecue. He made a fire. He roasted the woman. As he roasted her, the woman got all wrinkled and twisted over the fire. She turned black. Her eyes were half open. She looked horrible. He tied her up in *mamure* cane like a piece of game. Then he hung her in the cane from the top of *Faru hidi* overlooking Lake Akuena.

"Okay," he said. "Now I'll bring you back to life."

He went back to Earth, to Wade's house. He went to return his hair, his head, his teeth. He took his own head back again. He thanked Wade for his help. As payment, he built him a new house in Truma achaka. It was huge. Some say it was the best house on Earth. Wade was a very wise man, a good friend to Wanadi. That's why he made that house for him.

Then he called Kadiio, the squirrel. He told him to climb the tree and cut the cane Kaweshawa was hanging from.

Wanadi sent him to free Kaweshawa so she would fall into Lake Akuena. Then she'd come out new and beautiful again, just like in the beginning.

Now Kadiio climbed up the *Faru hidi* tree. He was like a man when he climbed up. He had good teeth. He had to cut the cane with those teeth. When he got up to Heaven, he looked around. When he looked, he saw Kaweshawa tied up there, all bent and twisted and making horrible faces. She was ugly. Then he burst out laughing. "That's Wanadi's woman," he said. And he rolled on the ground with laughter. He couldn't stop laughing. He just went on laughing and laughing. His teeth fell out from all that laughing. He couldn't cut anything. He couldn't do a thing. He went back down laughing and turned into a squirrel.

Today's squirrels took his form later on. That's why they only have two teeth in their mouth.

"You're worthless," Wanadi said to him. "You didn't do anything. You can stay that way without any teeth."

Now he called Anteater. He was like a man in the beginning. He had all his teeth. When he got up there, he looked around. "She's so ugly, she makes me laugh." he said. And he laughed and laughed just like the other one. His teeth all fell out too. He couldn't cut. That's why his children, the anteaters, have no teeth now. That's what the old ones say.

When he came down, he was still laughing.

"You didn't do anything," Wanadi said. "You can stay without teeth too. You didn't do what I told you to. You're worthless."

Now Wanadi called Kasuwaraha, the lizard. In those days, he looked like a person. He dashed up to the top of the tree. He didn't laugh. He cut.

Kaweshawa fell like a bundle of bones and burnt flesh. She fell right into Lake Akuena. As she fell, she broke her arm. It split into two pieces. Now she came out of the water, beautiful and new. Not one Kaweshawa, but two. There were two born from Akuena; one from each of the two parts of the old Kaweshawa. Another woman was born from the broken arm, just like the other one, but much smaller. Kasuwaraha went back to Earth with the two women.

"You're good," said Wanadi. "Your children, the lizards, will run up trees just as fast as you did. They'll be safe from their enemies. They won't be able to catch them."

Wanadi looked at the two Kaweshawas. "Good," he said. "They're beautiful, just like in the beginning, as if nothing had happened."

Now he gave Kasuwaraha his reward. He gave him the little Kaweshawa. He kept the other one. That's how Lizard became Wanadi's brother-in-law and loyal friend. Wherever Wanadi went, Lizard followed, helping him, warning him when there was danger, when enemies were coming. That's the way they tell it.

Now Wanadi thought: "I can get married."

He finished the new house on Mount Kushamakari. Then he went to get his in-laws at the old house in the water at Kasuruña Rapids.

They rejoiced when he told them: "Come now. The new house is ready. We'll go live together in Kushamakari. Today I get married."

Okay. That's all of it.

IUREKE

NUNA

That man, Attawanadi, found very few people on the Earth when he came. They were all under Odosha.

He told Nuna, the moon: "I'm going to make people. I'll go back to Heaven and ask for *Huehanna*."

"Good," said Nuna. "I want people too."

"Okay," he answered. "When I get that *Huehanna*, I'll give you your own people."

"Good," he said. Now he thought to himself: "How many people is he going to give me? I better go get *Huehanna* myself."

He was a *huhai*. He went up to Kahuña, to the highest part, up to the door of the Wanadi from there. It never opens. No one goes in the house. No one sees Wanadi. You can only speak with the guards at the door.

Nuna lied when he got there. "I'm Wanadi, the one from the Earth," he said. "I came for *Huehanna*. I'm going to make people there."

The guards told Wanadi: "Attawanadi's here. He wants *Huehanna*."

"Okay," said Wanadi. The guards called Nuna to the door and they gave him *Huehanna*.

Now Nuna went back down, happy. He wanted people like Wanadi, but just to eat them. He was hungry. He was evil. He thought like Mado, the jaguar: "There's no food. Okay. I'll eat people."

That's the way his evilness got started.

Now Attawanadi arrived. "I want to make people on Earth. I want *Huehanna*."

The guards said: "Again? We just gave it to you."

"I don't know," he answered. "I don't know anything."

"We gave it to you," they said. And they didn't give him anything.

He went back down to the Earth again, thinking: "They've been tricked. Someone stole *Huehanna*."

When Nuna got home, he thought: "I'm going to eat." That man's sister lived in the same house. She was a beautiful, young girl. Her name was Frimene.

"Where were you? What's that?"

"In Kahuña," he said. "That's *Huehanna*."

"It's beautiful. It looks like a tinamou egg," the girl said.

Huehanna was buzzing like a beehive. People were dancing and singing in there. You could hear voices.

"I want it!" the girl thought. "It's filled with people who haven't been born." She knew Nuna had stolen it.

"I can't let him eat them. I'll save them. I'll keep them myself. I don't want to give them back to Wanadi. I'm going to raise them. I'll hatch them. I'll be their mother." That's what the girl thought to herself when she saw *Huehanna*. She didn't say anything; she just thought it.

Now Nuna said: "I'm going over there. Keep *Huehanna* in the house. Watch it. Wanadi may come looking for it. If he comes, say: 'I don't know anything. I haven't seen a thing.'"

"Okay," said the sister.

When the man left, the girl hid *Huehanna* in her vagina, thinking: "It's done. I'll keep them all in my belly. They'll be born. I'm going to be their mother." She rubbed her stomach. She was happy. She listened to the dancing and the shouts of laughter of Wanadi's little people. They were going to populate the Earth.

When the man returned, he looked for *Huehanna*. It wasn't there. He got angry, really angry.

"Did Wanadi come? Did he take it?"

"I haven't seen anyone," she said. "I don't know anything."

He beat her. Then Nuna saw his sister's stomach. It was round as if she were pregnant. He just looked and looked. He knew what it was. He didn't say anything.

She turned her back. She didn't want him to hear or see. "I'm going," she said. "I'm tired. I'm going to get in my hammock."

She left. Night came. Now she was alone. She listened to her stomach. She listened to the voices and the drums, the songs and the horns. It was her children. She fell asleep.

Then she woke up. She opened her eyes. She couldn't see anything. There was no sun. Everything was dark and quiet. She heard a dull sound, very faintly. It was like steps. They were coming closer. She couldn't see. She just heard them. She was frightened. "Who could it be?" she thought. The steps were coming toward the hammock. They were coming very, very slowly.

When they arrived, a big object, like a body, fell on the hammock. It was a man. That girl was scared. He didn't say anything.

She didn't hear anything. Hands were moving all over her, landing here and there like bees on the girl's body. They were feeling and groping and searching. You could just barely hear *Huehanna* softly humming below. The girl squeezed her legs shut to protect her children. The hands tried to spread them. Impossible. They couldn't.

The sun hadn't come up when that man jumped out of the hammock and went away. He didn't say anything, just that sound, like very, very slow steps. Now the sun rose. Then the girl got up.

"What happened?" she thought. "Was it a dream? Who was it? Odosha? Wanadi looking for his children? Nuna hungry? Now I'm going to find out."

She went to find some *caruto* oil. She put it in a gourd.

Now, in memory of that time, our women paint the inside of their gourds with *caruto*.

When night came, the girl painted herself. She painted her face, her legs, her entire body with *caruto*. She turned black with *caruto*. Then she got in her hammock and went to sleep.

When she woke up, she heard the steps in the dark. They were slowly coming toward her again. The man fell on her. Hands were feeling and groping and searching. They took hold of the girl's legs. They wanted to force open the cave. They wanted *Huehanna*. The girl squeezed her legs shut. The people inside *Huehanna* were spun around. A hand reached up. It touched *Huehanna*. It tried to grab it. The girl fought back. She started to bleed. She bled a lot.

That's why our women bleed each time Nuna passes, as a reminder.

When the sun came up, the girl jumped out of her hammock. She was alone again. "Now I'm going to find out," she thought. She went out to look.

On her way, she met her brother, hidden in a field, crouched down beside a trap.

"What are you doing?" she asked.

"Don't make any noise," he answered. "I'm hunting. I'm hungry. Some people are coming."

He was hunting people as if they were animals.

As he spoke, he showed his face. It was stained with *caruto,* his body too. His hands were all black with *caruto.*

"It was him," the girl said to herself. "I've found him out."

She didn't say anything. She just left.

Now that girl thought: "I can't live in Nunaña anymore."

She went back home. She gathered up her things and she fled.

Now Nuna has a stained face. When it's full, we look at the moon. We can still see those stains on his face. They're a reminder of the beginning. I've seen them. You can too.

That's the way the old ones tell it. Okay.

HUIIO

That woman fled into the jungle, her children in her stomach, her arms filled with gourds and baskets. She was running. As she ran, she dropped a gourd. When it hit the ground, it turned into Wiwiio, the tree duck. Another one fell. It turned into Kahiuwai, the anhinga. That's the way they were born. The woman went on running and came to the Uriñaku (Orinoco). She couldn't get across it.

"Okay," she said. "I can't get across. The water will be my path."

She went into the water. She fled from her brother's house swimming.

She said: "I'm the Water Mistress, the River Mother." Then she changed into Huiio, the Great Snake, the Water Mistress. She went beneath the water and hid. You couldn't see her anymore. Now she built her house at the bottom of the rapids.

The Orinoco had just been born. All the rivers were just starting to flow then. Marahuaka had just been cut down. Now Huiio was born. She made herself mistress of the new water which was flowing everywhere.

Wanadi was angry. His *Huehanna* had been stolen. He went looking for it. He asked the people. He went around asking. No one knew.

He went to Nuna's house. He asked him about *Huehanna*. "I don't know where it is," Nuna said. "My sister knows. She has it hidden in her stomach. That's why she ran away at dawn." That's what Nuna told Wanadi. He told him to get back at her. He thought: "This way she'll be punished."

Wanadi went to find the girl. He called everywhere for her. She didn't answer. He asked the people. "We haven't seen her," they said. Each one went on his way, looking and calling. Nothing. Then they got tired. They couldn't find her. They came back.

Wanadi had a brother. His brother's name was Müdo. When he wanted to, he turned into a great potoo.

"You're engaged to her," Wanadi said. "She'll come out if you call her. Then we can catch her."

"She's beautiful. With my big bill and tiny little eyes, she doesn't want me. I'm ugly. She's not going to come out if I call her."

"Let's try," said Wanadi. "I don't want to lose *Huehanna*. Help me."

"Okay, brother," Müdo answered. He called his friend Höhöttu, the owl. "Help me," he said. "Let's call her."

They both turned into night birds. They called and shrieked the entire night. When the sun rose she came out. She lifted her body out of the water, up above the river, high in the air, saying: "Here I am." But it wasn't the girl who came, it was the Great Snake, Huiio.

"Who are you?" asked Müdo. "I don't know you. I didn't call you." And he squinted his eyes to get a better look at her.

"Sure you called," she answered. "I'm her, your betrothed. That's why I came. I recognized your call."

When she came out, they heard the music from *Huehanna*. You could hear those children of Wanadi's singing and dancing inside the snake's belly. They were waiting to come out.

Müdo said to the Great Snake: "Wanadi wants you to give *Huehanna* back."

"I can't," she answered. "I have my children in it."

"They're not yours. They're Wanadi's."

She didn't want to give them back.

Now Müdo and Höhöttu called the people, yelling in every direction. Many came. They made bows and arrows and spears. Müdo and Höhöttu were giving everyone orders. "We'll catch her and kill her," they said.

Now the first hunt began, when they chased Huiio along the river. They could see the rainbow, the snake's feather crown, from far off. She was spreading her feathers in the air, drying them in the sun. "There she is!" the hunters shouted. They were looking at the rainbow.

They were close now. They spoke to Dede, the bat. "We're going to shoot our arrows," they told him. "We're going to kill the snake and get *Huehanna* out. You stay here and just watch quietly. When *Huehanna* drops, catch it, so it doesn't fall in the water."

"Okay," said Dede. "I'll wait right here."

The hunters went to shoot the Great Snake. There were really a lot of them. They all shot at the same moment. Their arrows flew. Now Huiio looked like a porcupine with all those arrows stuck in her body. She fell over. She let go of *Huehanna. Huehanna* shot up in the air. Dede was watching, ready to catch *Huehanna* with his fishnet so it wouldn't fall.

"Grab it!" they shouted. "Don't lose it!"

Now Ficha, the cuckoo, came zooming up, headed straight for Dede. He had a long tail. He shoved Dede aside with that tail and took the fishnet.

"Move over," he said. "Let me get it. Your eyes are too small. You can't see."

Ficha was vain and wild. No one could tell him anything. He did whatever he wanted to. That's why the accident happened.

As he took the net, *Huehanna* was coming by. He tried to catch it. There wasn't time. *Huehanna* flew right by. It fell in the water.

"It's gone!" they all screamed. "Because of you, we've lost it!"

There was a huge rock in the water. *Huehanna* burst on it. The unborn people flew all over. They didn't drown. They just turned into fish eggs. When the eggs opened, hundreds of fish came swimming out. They were the first ones. Crocodiles came out too, and caimans and anacondas; all the animals you see today living in the rivers and lakes. Huiio was the mother of them all. They killed her. She collapsed on the shore. She died there, covered with arrows.

She didn't really though. She was too powerful. She just left her form, her body here. The rainbow is a reminder. Now she lives in the highest Heaven, in Lake Akuena. Now she's the mistress of Akuena, of eternal life.

Her body remained on Earth as a great snake. They ate it. First came a jaguar named Manuwa. He took the first bite. His mouth was full of blood.

"*Taduiche! Taduihena!* I haven't eaten! I'm hungry!" the others screamed when they saw the blood.

They hadn't eaten meat yet. They had cut down Marahuaka. They had only eaten yuca and fruit. Now they started to hunt, that day that they ate meat. One after the other, they all came, right down to the smallest one, shoving and pushing to get a mouthful.

"*Taduiche! Taduihena!*" we hunters scream now. We always remember the first hunt, the death of Huiio.

When Huiio died, the rivers overflowed their banks. They flooded the villages. They flooded the entire Earth. The people fled, running to the cliffs and the caves in the mountains. When the Great Water went down again, they thought: "We can go back now. There's no more danger."

Then they went back and ate the Great Snake, the Water Mother.

Müdo and Höhöttu, the night birds, were those people's chiefs in the beginning. They gorged themselves with meat and went off one after the other. The blood-stained river was full of fish now. Wanadi's people weren't born; they were turned into fish.

The sun went down. Only Manuwa the jaguar and his woman were left. The woman was looking at the blood on the rocks by the shore. She found two fish eggs that were still dry. They had fallen on the rocks and hadn't opened.

"Those two escaped," said Manuwa's woman. "I'll take care of them. I'm going to hatch them. I'll be their mother."

"Good," said Manuwa. "That way we'll have people. We'll have meat at the house."

Manuwa's woman was called Kawao. She saved them both. Later, two boys were born. They were Huiio's children, brothers of those fish people.

That's what they say. That's how the old ones tell it. That's all now.

KAWAO

A long time ago, the people didn't know about fire. They ate their food raw.

A woman had the fire. She kept it hidden in her belly. She didn't show it to anybody, not even her husband. The woman was named Kawao. Whenever she wanted to, she turned into a toad. Her husband's name was Manuwa. When he went out to hunt, he changed into a jaguar. He ate humans.

Kawao knew the secret. She cooked like our women do now. She fried yuca, manioc, cassava; she boiled fruit; she roasted meat. She would hide whenever she did it. She waited till Manuwa went out hunting. When she was all alone, she opened her mouth and pulled the fire out of her stomach. She'd spit fire under the food like that. Then she pulled in her tongue and swallowed the fire again. Then her husband came home. His food was ready.

When he came in, he asked: "How'd you do it?"

He didn't know.

"With the heat of the sun," the woman answered. "I just put the food in the sun, that's all."

"Oh," said that jaguar. He was very simple-minded. The woman had him fooled.

The day they killed Huiio, the Water Mother, Kawao found two fish eggs. They were abandoned by the shore.

"Take them," her husband said.

"Okay," she answered, and she took them home.

She wanted to hatch them in order to have children. He wanted children too, so he could eat them.

When she got home, she put the eggs near the hearth. It was a secret hearth. She blew her fire out there. The fire's heat opened the eggs.

They weren't fish that were born; they were boys. The eldest one was named Shikiemona; the younger, Iureke.

They were two powerful men. They grew very fast after they were born. Right away, they walked. They talked. They ate. They weren't children anymore. They were the fish's brothers but they looked like people. They came out of *Huehanna* with the fish. Kawao, the toad, found them. She adopted them.

"I'm your mother," she told them. She didn't tell them the true story, about their mother, about their mother's death.

They were wild, unruly kids. They ran all over shouting and screaming and fighting. They raised a terrible ruckus. They asked question after question. They were pests. They changed their forms every other minute. They played pranks on people just for the fun of it. First they were boys, then fish, then crickets, then cockroaches. They made fun of Kawao. They didn't pay any attention to her. It was like four hundred kids inside that house and there were only two.

They liked going in the river.

"That's not good," said Manuwa. "The fish will say something. They'll tell them the truth."

"Okay," said Kawao. "I'll forbid them to go in."

When they returned, she told them: "I don't want you to go in the water anymore."

"Okay, mother," they said. "We won't go back."

Then they asked for their dinner. Kawao sent them out to play. "I want to be in here alone to cook."

"Okay," they said. "We'll go." But they stayed.

Then they said: "Tell us how you do it."

"With the heat of the sun," she answered.

"No, it couldn't be with the heat of the sun," they said. "You can't. Tell us the truth now."

The woman got angry. She threw them out of the house. "Now you'll be punished. I won't give you any food."

They came in another door. "Give us cassava," they said. "Tell us how you do it."

Kawao gave them a beating.

When they left, they jumped in the water saying: "Okay, we won't go back. We'll never go back."

They went down with the fish, swimming just like fish. At the bottom of the river they came to an enormous house. They called out. Nothing. No one answered.

"This house is empty," they said.

Then they went in.

"Nice house," said the older one.

"I feel like I've been here," answered the other.

They found two hammocks. They got in and went to sleep. As they slept, they dreamed. They saw Huiio in the dream.

The Great Snake said: "This is my house, your house. I'm your mother. Wanadi is your father. They've lied to you. That's not your house. The toad isn't your mother. The jaguar isn't your father. They killed and ate me. I live in Kahuña now. I just speak to you in dreams. Be careful with the jaguar. He wants to eat you. You'll have to kill him first."

That's what the two twins dreamed when they slept on the river bed, in Huiio, their mother's house.

When they woke up, they found a gourd filled with *caruto* oil. They picked it up. Now they dreamed again.

"This was my gourd, my *caruto shimi* for painting myself. If you throw it out, the rivers will overflow. Water will cover the Earth. You'll drown the people. The people that came to kill me were many. They came from all over, down to the smallest one. They all ate me."

The boys woke up again. "Okay," they said. "One day we'll avenge our mother. We'll flood the entire Earth. We'll drown all the people. We'll come back here and get the gourd."

Then they hid it and swam away, saying: "Let's go back to Toad and Jaguar's house. They're not our parents. We'll fool them. We'll punish them for our mother's death."

On their way they came to a rock. They got out there and rested, like boys again. Above the rock, there was a tree. A beautiful branch was hanging down from it. There were beautiful yellowtail nests hanging from the branch. Lots of yellowtails were coming and going.

Now the boys were looking at one of the nests. Konoto, the father of the yellowtails, was poking his head out of the nest's entrance.

"Here we are," said Iureke. "Do you live here on the river? Tell us how Huiio, the mother of the fish, was killed."

Konoto answered, *"Tiwa, tiwa."* That's the way he sang. That's the way Konoto sings today too. You can hear him.

"What did you say?" asked Iureke.

"*Tiwa, tiwa,*" he sang again.

"I don't understand yellowtail talk," said Iureke.

"I understand," said Shikiemona. "He's saying '*tiwa, tiwa*'. Shooting, shooting."

That's the way the boys learned how their mother had died. When they got back to Manuwa's house, they didn't go in. They just put their ears against the door and listened.

"They went back to the river," said Kawao. "They don't listen. They just pester me with all their questions."

"They're big now. If they discover the truth, they'll kill us. If they come back, kill them. Cut off their heads with the scissors." Manuwa said.

"How can I do it? I raised them. They're my children now," Toad answered.

"I'm going out now to find *medikiu* to salt them with. Make a broth! Season it well! Get the meal ready! I'm going to look for *medikiu*. I'll be back soon. I'll be hungry," said Jaguar. He went out to find ash to salt the boys' soup with.

"Okay," said Kawao.

Now the boys came in through the other door.

"We're here," they said. "We've been swimming. We're hungry now. Where's our dinner?"

"There's no food," Kawao answered.

"We're hungry," they said. "Give us some cassava. Tell us how you make it."

"No. You don't listen," answered Toad. She gave them a whack and threw them out.

"Okay, we're going," they said.

The boys left. Now they made a plan.

"What should we do?" one of them said.

"We'll discover the secret," said the other. "We'll steal it. We don't want to be cooked in that soup."

"Okay," said Iureke. "We'll go back again and ask for our dinner. She'll throw us out. I'll hide inside the house. You go outside and make a lot of noise. She'll think we're playing. I'll be hidden in the roof, watching. That's how we'll find out."

They went in. They asked for cassava. Kawao threw them out.

Only Shikiemona left. Iureke hid in the roof. He wanted to find out

Toad's secret. He took out one of his eyes. He stuck it in the back of his neck to see behind him. Kawao heard the noise Shikiemona was making outside. It sounded like two boys playing. It was only one.

"Good. They're gone," Kawao thought. "They're wrestling now. I'll make cassava. I better hurry before they come back in and bother me."

Now she went to find her pan. Iureke's reflection was in it. She turned her head toward the roof. Iureke was up there.

"What are you doing up there on the rafters? Didn't you go out with your brother to play? Get out. I want to be alone. I'm going to cook now."

"I can't," said Iureke. "I lost an eye. I can't see very well. I can't walk. I won't watch you. I'll turn around and face the ceiling."

"Turn around then," the woman said. "Don't watch me," she told him.

"Okay," he answered. The boy turned around. "I can't see anything. Go on and cook now. We're hungry." He could see everything through the eye in the back of his neck. That's the way he tricked her. She opened her mouth. She blew fire under the pan. It was really bright under the pan. The eye behind Iureke's head was blinded. He couldn't see anything anymore.

Now Shikiemona came up to the door. "I want to come in now," he said.

The food was ready. Kawao shot out her tongue and scooped up the fire. She swallowed it. She hid it in her stomach again.

"Come in," she told Shikiemona. "Come down again," she told Iureke.

The boy took the blinded eye out of the back of his neck. He put it in front again. He could see fine once it was back in place. He could see the grilled manioc ready to be eaten.

Then the boys asked: "How did you make this food? Give us a taste."

Kawao started hitting them. She wanted to eat alone, in peace. Then she ate without giving them any.

Shikiemona whispered to his brother: "What happened?"

"I saw the thing," Iureke answered. "It burns. It shines like the sun. It's beautiful . . . gorgeous."

"Let's steal it," they said. "Let's take it from her."

Now the woman came up with the scissors. "Your hair is really long, boys. Come here. I'm going to cut it."

"Okay, mother," they answered and walked over quietly. They didn't say anything now. They were very still.

Kawao didn't want to cut off their hair. She wanted to cut off their heads. She started cutting their hair. At first it made her sad. Her hand shook. Then she thought: "My husband told me to. He'll be back soon. He'll be hungry. He'll ask for his meat broth."

She spread the scissors around Shikiemona's neck. Iureke leapt up. He pulled the scissors away. He jumped on Toad.

Now the two of them began kicking her and cutting her with the scissors. They squeezed her stomach. They opened her mouth.

They both screamed: "Throw it up! Take that thing out of your stomach!"

Kawao began to cough and spit. She choked. She was suffocating. Now the fire got caught in her throat. It was stuck. It wouldn't come out. The boys squeezed. Nothing.

"Spit it out! Throw it up!" they screamed, kicking and cutting her.

She coughed. She couldn't get it out. The lump of fire got up to her throat. It swelled. It went back down. It wouldn't come out.

"Vomit! Spit it out!" they screamed.

Then Shikiemona split open Toad's mouth. The fire gushed out. It burned Toad's back. It rolled onto the floor. Iureke pounced on it. He caught it.

"You let it out!" they screamed. "You threw it up!"

Because of that, the toads today, Kawao's grandchildren, all have wrinkled backs and wide mouths. They have a lump in their throat. It goes up and down.

Kawao's head was hanging from the slit in her mouth. They gave it a little tug. The head fell off. That's the way that Toad died.

" 'Cut their heads off with the scissors!' We did like Manuwa said," said the boys, and they rocked with laughter.

" 'Make a broth! Season it well! Get the meal ready!' Now we'll do just what Manuwa said." And they fell down laughing.

They cut up Toad. They blew fire under the pot. They picked up the head. They put it on the bottom and the other pieces on top. Then lots of chili peppers. Now the pot sang. Bubbles formed in the broth as the boys cooked.

They heard steps on the path as Manuwa came back. They got up in a hurry. They hid the fire. They looked around for a spot.

"Here? There?"

"No, there. Here's not good."

There were two trees behind the house. Wishu is the name of one; Kumnuatte the name of the other.

They hid it. Iureke hid one half in Wishu. Shikiemona the other half in Kumnuatte. We always remember that when we want new fire. We take Wishu and Kumnuatte and we rub them against each other, calling all the time. Right away, the fire jumps out. It shines. Those boys kept it for us. They hid the fire in two trees in the beginning. Because of that, people eat well now.

That's all.

MANUWA

"I smell some good soup," said Manuwa.

He was carrying *medikiu* as he came in. Because he was in his house now, that Jaguar changed into a person. Now the boys, Iureke and Shikiemona, changed into crickets. They hid inside the hearth. They started singing like crickets.

The pot was singing. Manuwa sniffed it. "It's ready," he thought. He tossed a handful of *medikiu* salt in the pot. Then he said: "I'm hungry."

He called his woman. He called. He looked. He called again. Nothing. "She's gone out," he thought. "Okay, I'm going to eat these boys."

He pulled out a piece, then another and another. He ate. "Delicious," he said. "These boys are delicious."

They came out of the hearth. Now they were two cockroaches. They ran. They climbed right up that man's leg. One on each leg.

The man let out a curse and slapped his legs. He threw the cockroaches off. Now they fell down. Right away, they climbed up his back. They went into his ears. One in each ear. He shook his ears. He cursed and screamed. He got the cockroaches out. They came back again. They covered his eyes. A cockroach on each eye. He snorted. They went up his nose. He sneezed. They fell out. He wanted to crush them. They turned into crickets. They hopped away. They hid in the hearth.

"Okay," that man thought. "They're gone. I can go on eating."

The food was almost all gone. He pulled out the last piece. It was his wife's head.

He let out a scream when he saw that head; a jaguar scream. The whooooole house shook. He went crazy when he figured out the boys' trick.

Now he feels something tickling. He shakes his legs. Two cock-roaches fall off. He tries to crush them. They get away. They run up the center post. They hide in the roof.

Now that man squats down. He looks up at the roof and waits. "They'll come back down," he says. They didn't.

"They'll come down soon," he said. He went to get a club. He came back and sat down at the foot of the post to wait. He just kept watching and watching. He fell asleep watching. When he fell asleep, the two cockroaches came tip-toeing down. They were like two boys again. They took the man's club. They ran away.

As he slept, the man dreamed: "They killed my wife. Now they're stealing my club. Now they're walking in the forest. I'm going to find them."

He woke up. He raced out. He went out like a jaguar to hunt them.

They weren't far off. He found them right away, up in a *wasai* palm. The *wasai* was full. Jaguar turned his head to look at them. The boys were up above. They were eating fruit. They were laughing.

"You made it," they said when they saw him.

"Here I am," he answered. "What are you doing up there?"

"Just eating. Delicious food. You want some?"

"Yeh, I want some too."

"Okay," they said. "Here comes your food."

They cut Jaguar off a branch.

"Open your mouth," they shouted.

They dropped the branch. It fell right on his head. Jaguar didn't eat. He was sprawled out with his legs open.

The boys came down laughing. They quickly ran off.

Manuwa wasn't dead. He pulled a new jaguar out of his body. That's how he chased the boys again. That Manuwa had power. Those boys couldn't kill him.

Then he found them again, up in a tree once more. He sat down at the foot of the tree.

"Now what are you doing?" he said to them.

"Eating honey," they said.

"I want some too," he answered.

"Delicious honey," they said. "You want some?"

"Yes, I want some!"

"Here it comes. Open your arms, your mouth."

That Jaguar was dumb. They tricked him. They just cut off the honeycomb to fool him. They weren't eating it. It was hot honey. It wasn't sweet. It was like fire. They threw it down. He swallowed it. He choked. He coughed. He wept. He fell over.

"He's dead," they said, laughing.

Then the boys went off laughing and playing, to find more food.

Jaguar was mad. "Now I'll catch them. Now I'm going to eat them." He didn't get very far because on his way he met Waiamo, the turtle.

Now we'll tell how Turtle fooled that Jaguar. Everyone was fooling him.

Waiamo was out hunting. He got hold of an enormous tapir. The tapir got loose. Waiamo jumped up. He snapped at him. He caught him. He bit onto his penis. He wouldn't let go. The tapir took off running and screaming: "Let me go! Let me go!" He just squeezed tight and hung on. "Let me go! I'm dying!" said the tapir as he went on running, and then he died. Now Waiamo was ready to let go. He couldn't.

He was hanging from that dead tapir's penis when Jaguar arrived. He said to him: "Help me. Cut off the penis. I can't let go."

"Okay," said Jaguar. He cut it off.

Now Waiamo said: "Look how big that tapir is. I killed it."

"Good," said Manuwa. "I'm going to eat it."

"That is," the other answered, "*we're* going to eat it."

"No. I'm going to eat it," said Jaguar, giving Turtle a kick that sent him spinning on his back. Turtle moved his feet. Nothing. He couldn't set himself right.

"Turn me over," he said. "I'm upside down. Give me another kick."

"First I'm going to eat," said Jaguar. "Then I'll set you right." He took a bite out of the tapir.

Waiamo thought: "How am I going to do this?"

"Delicious tapir," said Manuwa as he went on eating.

Waiamo just lay there thinking with his feet sticking up. Then he said: "I'd eat it with chili peppers."

"What'd you say?"

"It's a shame to eat it that way. It's much better with chili peppers. Meat without chili peppers is terrible."

"Shut up. I don't have any peppers," said Jaguar. He went on eating.

"I have a beautiful *conuco* just filled with peppers," said Turtle.

"Really? Where is it?"

"Over there," he answered, moving his feet.

"Go get some," Jaguar said.

"I can't. I'm upside down."

Jaguar stopped eating. Then he said: "Tapir without chili peppers is terrible."

Now he gave Turtle his kick. He set him right.

"Go get that chili pepper. Run!"

"I don't know how to run," he answered. "We turtles don't know how."

He was silent. Then he said: "Do you know how to make a roast?"

"No," answered Manuwa.

"Okay. I do. That's the path to the chili peppers. I'm going to get them now. Wait for me. I'll come back with the peppers. Then I'll make a barbecue."

Jaguar waited. Turtle came back with the peppers. He made a barbecue. He fixed the hot sauce and put it in a gourd. Then he threw it right in Jaguar's face. The peppers burned his eyes. Now Turtle hid the meat in a cave. Then he went to hide in the cave with the meat.

"Where are you?" shouted Jaguar.

"Here. In the cave," he answered.

"Where are you?" Jaguar shouted. "I can't see you. I can't see anything."

"Here. In the cave."

Jaguar was mad. He stuck his foot in the cave. Nothing. It was narrow. He couldn't feel him.

His foot was wide. It couldn't get into the cave. Then Jaguar found a vine and stuck it in. Nothing. The vine was too short. He found another. Nothing. Then another. Nothing. Now he went and cut a really long vine. He poked it in here. He poked it in there.

"Now I'll get you out of that cave."

"What'll I do now?" thought Turtle. Then he said: "Okay. I'll roll it up."

Jaguar was sticking it in. He was rolling it up. The cave swallowed up the entire vine.

"Okay," said Jaguar. "That cave's too deep. I can't get him."

He forgot about the meat. He went to look for the boys again.

When he left, Turtle came out laughing. He was carrying the coiled vine and laughing. Then he turned into a boy and called his brother.

When Iureke called his brother, Shikiemona came.

"What happened?" he asked.

He told him everything and they fell down laughing.

Now they went off in one direction and Jaguar in another.

That's the way the old ones tell this.

Okay. Now we'll tell how Jaguar lost his eyes. He was stupid. Those boys were always playing tricks on him.

He went looking for them. They were on another trail. And so, one moon passed and then another and another.

Now those boys were in Sokoa tahu. It's a little island in the Orinoco near the Atabapo. They were sitting there playing with their eyes. They were sitting in front of each other tossing their eyes back and forth.

"Catch!" said one. He threw an eye to the other.

"Catch!" the brother answered. He threw his brother an eye.

Jaguar swam up. He was happy when he got there. "Here they are!" he said. "They can't get away from me on this little island."

"What's that?" he asked.

"We're airing out our eyes," they said. "We're just playing."

"Why are you throwing them around?" he asked.

"To see better," they said. "Fresh air's good for them."

Iureke took one out of his head. He threw it to Shikiemona. Then he caught his brother's eye. He stuck it in. Then the other eye. Shikiemona did the same thing. Two eyes flew by. Two eyes were still in each of their heads. That's the way those boys switched eyes.

"Okay," said Jaguar. "I want to do it. I want to see better too."

"They're dry now," they said. "They're clean. When we got up they were covered with dreams."

"I dreamed last night," said Jaguar. "I'm going to wash my eyes."

"Okay. Good," they said. "We'll do it for you. Hurry up and take them out."

He took them both out and gave them to the boys.

"Are they ready yet?" he asked. "I want my eyes."

"They're really dirty," they said. "They're covered with dreams. Just hang on a little."

"Okay. Enough!" said Jaguar. "Give me back my eyes."

The boys laughed as they tossed around his eyes.

"Okay. We'll give them to you," they laughed. "Here, catch."

"No, please!" said Jaguar.

"Okay," they said. "We'll put them out on this rock to dry now. They're shiny . . . beautiful. They're really clean. You'll be able to see a long ways for hunting."

Wadakane, the crab, came up.

"Give those eyes a little shove and turn them over," they told him. "They're only getting dry on one side."

Wadakane shoved the eyes. They began to roll.

"Pluup!" said the eyes as they fell in the water.

"They've fallen in!" Jaguar screamed, wanting to cry. But he couldn't. He didn't have any eyes. He stuck out his paw and tried to find them. He hit Wadakane right on the head and split open his skull.

Now crabs have split skulls. You can see them.

"Let's go fishing," said the boys. And they jumped in the water like two fish. They didn't come back.

Manuwa was left on Sokoa tahu alone. He couldn't cry. He just cursed.

Agouti came up.

"Here I am," he said.

"Who are you?" he asked. "I can't see. I can't see anything."

"It's Agouti. Here I am. Don't you want to eat me?"

"How can I eat you? I want you to help me. Two Odoshankomo have thrown my eyes away. They did it as a joke. They fell in the river."

Agouti looked at Jaguar. He was quite delighted. Whenever Jaguar had his eyes and was hungry, he never did anything but chase him and his family.

Agouti laughed. He wasn't afraid.

Now he turned around and said: "Here are your eyes." And he blew a horrible, smelly fart right in Jaguar's face. Then he left.

Manuwa sat there alone, thinking.

Then Karakaradi, the king vulture, came up. He was thin. He didn't have any food.

"Here I am," said Karakaradi.

"Who are you?" he asked. "I can't see you. I don't have any eyes."

"It's me, Vulture. I came to see what's going on. Why aren't you out hunting? I'm hungry. I can't find any carcasses."

Karakaradi always ate Manuwa's leftovers. Jaguar would eat and move on. Then Karakaradi would come.

"I'll go find you some new eyes," he said. He went away and came back with some wonderful eyes. He tried to shove them in. They wouldn't fit in that Jaguar's head. They were too big. Finally they went in.

Now Jaguars have great, brilliant eyes. They're good hunters too.

Jaguar jumped in the water and swam away. He was happy. He killed a deer and ate it. He left the carcass and the bones. That's the way he paid Karakaradi for his eyes. Then he found Agouti. He killed him. That's how he collected for that terrible fart.

"Okay," he said. "Now I'm going to find those boys."

They were swinging on a vine. The vine was hanging from a tall palm tree. They swung all the way out and all the way back, all the way out and all the way back.

"What's that?" he asked as he came up with his new eyes. He came to eat them. First he wanted to know what that game was.

"*Uauianatoho*," they said. "It's just a game."

"Why are you swinging?" he asked.

"To get strong. To get power. We swing all the way out and get the good wind. Then we bring it back."

"I'm really tired," said Jaguar. "I want some wind. I need some power."

"Okay," they said. "We'll help you if you want."

They came down from the vine. Then they stuck Manuwa up there. Now they began pushing. He swung out and back. He liked it.

"New air!" they said to him. "You're getting new power!"

"More!" said Manuwa.

They pushed him harder. He went way high up. Then he came back.

"You're flying!" they shouted. "You're going to come back with wind from the clouds!"

"Great!" he said. "More!"

"Okay," they said. "Now we'll send you to Akuena. You'll come back brand new, like a new born baby again."

They pushed him really hard. He flew way out, hanging on the vine. Now they raced up the palm tree. They cut the vine from above. He just took off and flew. He didn't come back again. First they threw away his eyes. Now they threw him away!

Manuwa was flying. He was flying through the clouds. The people looked up, screaming: "There goes a flying jaguar! It must be some powerful *huhai!*"

Manuwa thought: "I'm a *huhai*. I'm flying with my body. I'll be in Kahuña soon." He looked at the people, the rivers, the trees. They were tiny. He looked and laughed. He flew over the Kunukunuma, the Antawari, the Orinoco. He saw the villages all around. Then he saw strange rivers, new villages. "This must be the end of the Earth," he thought. "I'm entering Kahuña now."

Then the people started getting bigger. The rivers began to grow. The trees were falling on top of him. They were hitting him.

"I'm falling!" he screamed.

He was falling too.

He fell way far off there, at the edge of the Earth. He broke all his bones. He stayed there, recovering. He never found his way. He never came back. The boys never saw him again.

Okay, now. That's all.

AHISHA

White Man was in his canoe, fishing in the Manafiari. He was dressed in good clothes. Shirt, pants. He had a hat, and shoes too. His hook was good, made of iron. That man looked like Iaranavi. Actually, his name was Ahisha. He was the Great Egret. Whenever he wanted to, he turned into Iaranavi, into White Man.

Those boys came by. They were coming from Yaviña (Mt. Yavi). They had built a house in Yaviña.

"Let's go fishing," said one.

"Yeh, let's," answered the other.

They came to the bank. They saw Ahisha in the canoe.

"There's Iaranavi," said one.

"He has a good hook," said the other.

"Let's ask him for it."

They went up to the canoe. There was a little pile of hooks inside it.

"Here we are," they said.

"Okay," the man said. "But don't speak so loud. I'm fishing."

"You have good hooks!" they said, screaming. "Give us one. We're just some poor fishermen."

That man didn't want to. "Don't make so much noise," he said again. "I'm fishing."

"What is that?" they asked now, pointing to the hook.

"That's iron," that Iaranavi said.

"That's iron," they both repeated.

Then they left. They didn't say anything else.

They sat down on the riverbank, thinking. In those days, the people didn't know about iron.

"Okay," said one. "That man's no good. We'll steal the iron from him."

70

"How'll we do it?" asked the other.

The first one jumped in the water. He changed into a piranha. The other one jumped in too. He turned into another piranha.

They were brothers; Iureke, the younger one, Shikiemona, the eldest. That's what they were called.

Now two piranhas are playing near the hook, swimming around and around, watching that man's hook. Now one comes up to take a bite. He cuts the line. He carries off the hook.

"That piranha's cut my line," Ahisha said. "Hmm, I've lost the hook."

He took another from the canoe. He put it on the line.

Now he was quietly fishing again. They came back, swimming around and around.

"I'll bite it," said one.

It was Iureke.

"No, I'll get it," said Shikiemona.

He went up to cut it. He didn't bite right. He hooked himself.

"I've got you!" shouted the iron man, pulling his line in as fast as he could. He picked up the fish and threw him in a basket.

"Now you're punished," he said.

That's how Shikiemona stayed. He couldn't breathe. He was dying. Fish can't live outside of water.

"Okay," the other one thought. "How can I save him?"

He leapt out of the water. He came out flying. He was like Sakasakari, the kingfisher, now. He came down low and circled the canoe. He grazed the man's head. He flew over the basket of fish. Now he took aim. He dropped a big crap.

The man in clothes got angry. "That bird got my fish dirty." He bent down to wash it.

Right away, Shikiemona came to life again in the water. He slid away.

Ahisha was mad.

"Here you are," said Iureke. They were both in the water again, like piranhas.

"Be careful now. You can't cut. Stay here and let me do it."

That piranha went back. He stole another hook. Ahisha was furious. The piranha just kept coming back over and over again. That pile of hooks in the canoe disappeared. Ahisha was boiling.

"Okay," they said.

Now they both jumped into the canoe like boys. They were shouting and fighting with each other.

"Don't make so much noise!" the man screamed. He was really mad now.

"Give us an iron hook," they said.

"I don't have any!" he growled. "The piranha stole them."

Then he said: "I just have one left. Here, take it. Go away and leave me alone."

That hook wasn't iron. It was a thorn, just a fake one. That man just wanted the boys to leave him in peace. It seemed like they had been born just to bother people.

"Perfect," the boys said now. "This hook is really good. We'll definitely catch something. This is the best hook we've ever seen. Great! We'll catch tons of fish."

They wouldn't stop talking. They just went on and on, talking in circles. Pretty soon, they were fighting and screaming again. They were arguing over who was going to fish first. They wouldn't leave. They stayed there to bother that man.

Then Iureke threw his line in the water and caught a big pile of fish. He caught them instantly. He wasn't using the thorn but one of the good, stolen hooks.

Then Shikiemona caught a big pile too.

"Those two are *huhai*," thought Ahisha. Then he said: "You're good fishermen. Let's fish together, the three of us. We'll share our hooks and fish."

"Okay," they answered, and they immediately hauled in some more fish.

"Let's go to my house," said the man. "We can cook this there."

They made a *tudi*. They stuck the fish in. They loaded it on Iaranavi's shoulders.

That Iaranavi lived far away, over there in Ankosturaña.

The boys were walking in front; then the man with his load. It was heavy.

"You go in front now," they said. "We'll go behind to see that no fish fall out."

The man went on ahead. The boys weren't saying anything now.

"Why aren't you talking?" asked the man.

No one answered. He turned around to look. The boys weren't there anymore. "Good," he thought. "This is better. I'll keep all the fish myself."

Now he walked on alone. His basket wasn't that heavy anymore. He ran up to the house. He took off the basket. It was empty. On the bottom, two cockroaches were just finishing the last fish. He tried to kill them. Now they turned into two boys. It was Iureke and Shikiemona.

"Here we are," they said. Then they disappeared.

"Where'd they go?" asked the man. He was afraid now. Now his shirt and his pants started coming apart. They were falling off. Holes were forming all over them. They were like fishnets. Now the man was naked. Two moths came flying out. They circled around and disappeared. Ahisha let out a scream, not a man's but an egret's. He took his egret body and fled. He just flew away.

One moon passed and then another and another.

Ahisha, the egret, was in his house, quietly watching a hummingbird. His name was Tukui. He only drank flowers and nothing else.

"Where do you get this cloth and iron of yours?" that hummingbird asked.

"Oooowh, far away," said Ahisha. "On the edge of the ocean, in a beautiful village. It's called Amenadiña. I'm a traveller, a trader. I go there and buy. Then I come back and sell. Then I go and buy again. Then I come back and sell again."

"I want to go with you," he said. "I want to see Amenadiña and buy iron and cloth."

"Okay," said the man. "But it's very far. You're so little. I don't know if you can make it."

"I want to go," he said again.

"Okay, let's go," he answered.

That man turned into a great egret.

The two of them flew off; Egret in front, showing the way, Hummingbird following. They flew very slow because of Egret. Hummingbird got restless. He said: "Hurry up. I can't fly this slow." Then he said: "I know the way now. I'm going to fly ahead."

He sped off. Egret couldn't see him anymore.

Then Egret got hungry. He sat down on a tall mountain along the way to eat. That mountain was Marahuaka.

He opened his basket. He took out some fish. He made a barbecue and roasted them. Then he ate. While he was eating, Hummingbird arrived.

"You came back," he said to him.

"I came back," he answered. "That's too far. I'm tired. I'm sick. I have a fever and I'm starving to death. That's why I came back."

"Here's your food," he said, pointing to the fish.

Hummingbirds don't eat fish. They only drink flowers and nothing else. Tukui was dying of hunger. He just looked at the food. He didn't touch it. He just drank a little from a flower.

"What am I going to do?" he said. "I'm so tired. I can't fly without food."

"Sit on my feet. We'll go that way," said Ahisha. "With me flying and you sitting."

"Okay," he said. "I can do that."

And so that's the way they went to Amenadiña. Hummingbird fell asleep. Egret flew slowly, the way egrets do.

Then Egret woke Tukui up as they were flying. He said: "Watch out. I'm going to piss. I'm going to give you a bath now. If you want to keep going, hold on tight."

Then there was a big downpour. He really pissed a lot. He drenched Hummingbird, sitting on his leg in back.

Egrets piss the same way today, big downpours. You can see them.

Lighter now, he flew on. He just kept on flying and flying. Amenadiña was really far away. Hummingbird had a fever. He was starving and wet. He was sitting on that leg not moving at all. Then he fell asleep again.

When they got to Amenadiña, they saw that beautiful village there. They saw everything, the cloths, the iron, the rich people. Ahisha changed into a person, into Iaranavi. He bought lots of things. Tukui just watched. He couldn't move. He was almost dead.

"Okay," said Ahisha. "That's everything. Let's go back now."

He turned into Egret again. Then Tukui sat down again. They went back to Akosturaña.

When they arrived, Hummingbird said: "Good. Now I've seen Amenadiña. I'm going home now."

He flew back to his house in Yaviña. He turned into a boy there, like he really was. He was Iureke. His brother Shikiemona was in the house. He was waiting for him there.

"What happened?" he asked.

"I'm dying," he answered.

"Did you go with that Iaranavi to see the iron and cloth?"

"I went. I discovered his secret. There's a beautiful village far off there, on the edge of the sea. It's called Amenadiña. That's where the iron and cloth are. I saw everything there. I went as Hummingbird. He didn't recognize me. I couldn't eat because Hummingbird doesn't eat. That's why I got sick."

"Good. Now we know. We'll go there together. I want to see it too. Now you can eat like a person. You're not a hummingbird anymore."

He gave him fish. He stuffed himself. He felt better after he'd eaten.

They went to Ahisha's house together. One went as Shidishidi, the cockroach. The other as Wiha, the chiripa.

"We're here," they said. "When do you return to Amenadiña?"

"Well," said the man, "I'm going on the full moon."

"Okay," they said, and they scurried off.

The man filled his basket with cassava bread for the trip. He had lots of cassava to sell in Amenadiña.

Now the full moon came. He put on his basket. The two of them were there, hidden in the cassava. That man changed into an egret. He went flying off.

Night came. He set down on top of Marahuaka to eat and sleep. As he was sleeping, Cockroach and Chiripa ate the cassava. They made a lot of noise as they were eating in the basket.

Another night came. He set down on Dodoima to eat. Those two were really hungry. They didn't wait for him to go to sleep. They started eating his cassava right away. The cassava was crunching and making noise. "Chiripa," thought the man. He was really tired now. "I'll look later," he said. He fell asleep. Those two went on eating all night.

Ahisha woke up with the sun. He heard his cassava crunching, making noises. Then he opened the basket. He stamped on them. He cut off their heads. He tossed them away.

"Good," he said. "I killed them. I'm going now." And he packed up his cassava.

Cockroach and Chiripa left their bodies. They were *huhai*. They couldn't die. Now they came out as moths and got into that man's clothes.

When he changed into Egret to leave, they were in his feathers. That's the way they went to Amenadiña together. He didn't know it.

Ahisha bought many things in that village on the edge of the sea. He sold lots of cassava. He bought guns, machetes, knives, cloth, and lots of other stuff.

Those two just watched happily, in silence. They didn't buy anything.

Then they said: "Okay, we have enough now."

When Egret left, they hid in his feathers again. He was really tired when he got home. He took his Iaranavi body. He set down his basket. He lay down and went to sleep. The moths flew out of his shirt. They turned into boys. They took the basket and ran.

When they got back to Yaviña, they called all the people together. "We bought it in Amenadiña," they said. "We know the way." Everyone came to see the guns, the iron, the cloth. They were happy.

Now they divided everything between the people. Then they danced.

"We want to go too," everyone said.

"Okay. This is the way." They told them the way.

Before, the people didn't know it. Only Iaranavi knew that road. He was the iron man. Whenever our grandfathers wanted guns and machetes, cloth, glass beads, they asked Iaranavi. He used to sell them everything. Now they knew it too. They went to Amenadiña too. They forgot Iaranavi. They didn't go back to Ankosturaña.

The people of today remember. That's why we know the iron way, the cloth way. Those two boys discovered it in the beginning. It's a long, long way. Amenadiña is at the end of the Earth.

Now, that's all.

IUREKE'S WOMAN

Two brothers were living together. One had a woman. The other didn't. They were named Iureke and Shikiemona. Shikiemona was the single one.

Now the unmarried one fell in love with his sister-in-law.

"How will I do this?" he asked himself. His brother was watching him.

He went hunting in the mountains. He didn't come back. Then he sent a messenger to his brother.

"What happened?" Iureke asked the messenger.

"Your brother sent me. He can't walk. He says he's got niguas in his feet."

"Where is he?" asked Iureke.

"Way over there, all alone in the mountains."

"Okay, I'll send my wife."

The woman left right away with a needle to get the niguas out of his feet.

"Here I am," she said to her brother-in-law when she got there. "Where are the niguas?"

There weren't any niguas. Shikiemona jumped up with a smile on his face and ran toward her. He grabbed the woman. He carried her off deep into the forest.

Now when anyone tells a lie, we say: "Just like Shikiemona's niguas."

Iureke was thinking: "Why haven't those two come back? I'll go see what's wrong."

He went and found them. He was really mad. He beat his brother. He carried off his wife.

"Okay," said Shikiemona. "My brother hit me. I won't go back home. I'm going to go far away alone now."

He started walking. He walked all the way to the edge of the sea, to Amenadiña. He stayed there.

One moon passed, then another and another.

Now Iureke became sad. "My brother's angry. He went to live far away."

He sat down, elbows on his knees, head in his hands. He began to think and think.

Then he said: "Okay. We'll make peace. I'll send for him. I'll tell him to come back."

Iureke just sat there thinking in silence. He didn't eat anything. Then he said: "My brother's going to come back. I'll have to find food. We'll celebrate when he returns. Now I want to eat."

He was sitting, thinking, dreaming food. There wasn't anything in Yaviña, no trees, no fruit, no *conucos*. Now food sprang up there, when Iureke dreamed it. Now Yaviña is good earth.

He sent messengers. They walked and walked. That's how they got to Amenadiña.

"Your brother's calling you," they told that boy. "He's not mad anymore. He wants you to come back to Yaviña."

Shikiemona was afraid. "It's a trick," he thought. "Okay," he told them. "I'll return with the full moon." Then the messengers left.

Shikiemona gathered lots of people together. He didn't want to return alone. He was afraid. The people armed themselves like soldiers. Shikiemona went ahead to lead.

Iureke saw them as they approached. They were coming toward Yaviña, slowly climbing up Mount Yavi hidi.

Iureke thought: "What are all those armed men doing here? I only want peaceful people. I just want my brother."

They found lots of food and fruit along the path as they were climbing up. Iureke thought: "Now hot peppers." Now they ate hot peppers. All those who were coming to fight died. Shikiemona ate good food. He arrived at the house alone, with just a few peaceful people.

The brothers were really happy when they got back together again. Iureke called the people from every house on Earth to celebrate. They came from all over. Then he said: "We're going to have an enormous feast now. It's called *Wanwanna*."

We still celebrate *Wanwanna* now to remember. We remember the reconciliation, the peace, when Shikiemona returned home.

The men, women, and children come from all the houses on Earth.

The men bring game; the women manioc. There's lots of food. The men play. They wrestle. The women make *iarake* and cassava. The musicians come with *wanna* flutes, the dancers with palm skirts. It lasts for five days. They sing that *Wanwanna*. The first was in Yaviña, when Iureke forgave his brother.

Now that's how the old ones tell it. That's what they say.

DAMA

Iureke said: "Okay. The people are all together now. Everyone's here."

Shikiemona said: "Let's punish them now. When they killed our mother, they were all together too. They all ate her."

"Good," said Iureke. "We'll go get her *shimi* now."

They went in the water, down to the bottom of the river. They came to Huiio, the Water Mother's empty house. The *shimi* gourd with the *caruto* oil was hidden there. They took it back to the Earth. They threw it out. The rivers overflowed. Now it began to flood all over.

They took fire from the trees. They set fire to the houses. When the water came, the fire went out. The people were all together in Yaviña. They were all at the feast, drunk.

Now they shouted and screamed. They screamed and ran. The good people hid up in the mountains, in the cracks in the cliffs. They weren't many. The others all drowned. The houses fell down. The entire Earth was covered. They called that big water that came Dama (Sea). It didn't have any shores.

First they ran, those two boys. When they got to the headwaters of the Antawari, they were swimming like fish. You couldn't see anything but Dama. There was nothing left standing; houses, forests, mountains. Just two *moriche* palms were left. They went straight up, high, hiiigh, all the way to Heaven. The two boys climbed way up. They looked at Dama and rested.

The two *moriches* were like brothers, stuck right together. Now the boys made a platform way up high between the two. They both got on and sat down. Now they began eating *moriche* fruit. They just went on eating and eating, waiting for the Earth to dry.

As they ate they dropped the pits of those fruits down below there. First one day passed, then another and another.

Then Dama went far away. It went back to the horizon where our Earth ends. Now Dama starts there. It stayed there from that time.

"Let's go down," said the boys.

They climbed down.

When they got down, they stepped on soft earth. Their legs sank right into a swamp. That's all there was, just mud, nothing else.

Then the twin *moriches* turned into a huge stone. Now it's called Ekaui hidi, Moriche Mountain. It's there as a reminder, in the headwaters of the Antawari.

"Everyone's dead," they said when they came down. "No one's left. They've gotten their punishment for our mother's death."

Iureke said: "Good. Let's find their bones and skulls now. First Wanadi's and Müdo's, and Höhöttu's because they're the ones that told them to kill our mother."

They went off looking in the swamps with a *manare*. They strained the swamp through the *manare*. Skulls and little pebbles called *wiriki* stuck in the mesh.

They looked at the first skull. "This isn't it," they said. They looked at another. "Not this one." Another. "No." Another. "No." They went through a lot of skulls as they looked. They scoured the Earth, straining it. They didn't find what they were looking for.

Lots of bones and *wiriki* turned up in the *manare*. Those boys were looking for skulls. They didn't look at the *wiriki*. They just threw them away.

"They're worthless," they said when they threw them away. They didn't know. Those *wiriki* were power stones, wisdom stones. They were filled with the wisdom from the Sky. As they threw them away, the *wiriki* landed on the rock called Madan tahu. They shattered all over. Hundreds of little pieces came bouncing off. Now two people came up and started collecting them. They hadn't died. They escaped from Dama. Now they were quietly collecting *wiriki*. Those two men were named Maku and Fiaroa. They picked them up and kept them. They didn't leave one *wiriki* on the ground.

Now the two boys found the last *wiriki* in their *manare*. "Its worthless," they said. And they threw it away. It landed on Madan tahu. It burst. Maku and Fiaroa came to gather them. There were two pieces that landed far away. They couldn't find them. Those two pieces fell in the mouths of the two boys.

They liked them. They were good, sweet. "Mmmmm, these are good," they said. "Let's keep them."

It was too late. There were none left. They couldn't find any. Maku and Fiaroa had all the *wiriki*. Now they own the *wiriki*.

Those *wiriki* are the *tahuanohonato*, the *huhai's* wisdom stones. Because of those two boys, we were left without good, strong *huhai*.

The Makukomo and Fiaroakomo (Maku and Piaroa Indians) have all the powerful *huhai*. We don't know. We don't know their secrets. We just go and ask them for help.

That's what the old ones say.

The boys didn't find the skulls they were looking for.

Now they heard: "Woo woo woo," and then "Owo owo owo." They turned their heads. Müdo was up on a big rock quietly watching. Höhöttu was watching too, sitting there by his side. They were both fine. They were powerful. That's why Dama didn't kill them.

On another mountain they heard: "Tuk tuk tuk tuk." They saw Wanadi tonoro, the Wanadi bird, up there pecking on some wood. He was fine, as if nothing had happened.

"Okay," those boys said. They threw away their *manare*. They didn't look for any more skulls.

Then they met Tosede, the water hen. He was like a person walking along there with his rifle. He had his woman with him.

"How did you escape?" the boys asked him.

"In a gourd," they said. "We got inside a gourd."

"What are you doing with the rifle?"

"Hunting, hunting curassow, that's all."

Then they heard curassow singing. Then they heard more singing, and more and more and more. The boys just listened. They didn't say anything. Then they took Tosede's rifle away from him.

That's the way the old ones tell it. Many people died because of Dama. A few were saved. These were the good ones. They hid in the mountains, in gourds.

Those boys punished the bad ones. But they couldn't kill Wanadi, Müdo, or Höhöttu the way they wanted to.

Now there were only a few people left on the Earth. The boys said: "It's done. Let's go now." They left our Earth and went back to Heaven.

"Okay," Wanadi thought. "Only a few people are left. Okay, I'll make new people."

That's it.

KASENADU

DINOSHI

In the beginning the people were afraid of Lightning, Flash, and Thunder. They didn't know what it was. They just saw Lightning far away, heard Thunder far off.

There was a man, master of Lightning, Flash, and Thunder. He spent his time hunting in the mountains. When he hunted, that man would hide. Then Lightning shot out. No one saw him. No one knew how he did it. He didn't kill animals with arrows or spears like other hunters.

That man had a *conuco* full of yuca. He didn't want to let his sister take yuca from the *conuco*. "If you go back and take it, I'll punish you," he told her.

The sister went back to the *conuco*. That man got mad.

Dawn came and he left to go hunting in the mountains. He took his two little nephews. They were his sister's children. Now he took the children to the headwaters of the Wiwe in the Antawari Mountains. When they were far away there, that man shot out Lightning. He killed the children. He carved them up like animals. He opened them up and pulled out their hearts.

Then he put the two hearts on a frying pan. He stuck them up in the fork of a very tall tree called Kudi.

Now those hearts turned into two little harpy eagles. Right away they started to grow. Now they became huge. They had hooked beaks, curved claws, blood-stained eyes. They looked at that man. He looked at them too out of the corner of his eye. He was really scared now.

When those harpies were born, Kudi turned into an enormous mountain called Kudi huha. You can still see it as a reminder in the headwaters of the Wiwe. They had their nest on that mountain.

"They're going to come for me. They're going to eat me," thought that man. "I better kill them right now."

He shot Lightning at them. Nothing. Lightning just bounced off. Those birds had armor, like iron. Lightning didn't do anything.

Now the man started running. He ran for his life and didn't look back. He ran all the way back to his house.

When he got there, Enneku, his woman, asked: "What happened?"

"I found two baby harpy eagles in the mountains. They wanted to catch me," said Lightning Man. That was his name, Kasenadu.

"Good," said Enneku. "Why didn't you bring them home? I want to raise them. Go back and get them."

Kasenadu didn't want to. He was afraid.

"Okay," he answered. "If you want to raise them, you can go get them yourself."

Enneku went to Kudi huha alone. When she got there, two giant harpy eagles were watching her. They rushed out of that nest and picked her up. Then they ate her.

They were called Dinoshi. Now the two of them went flying over the Earth, over the roads, the houses, the *conucos,* looking for people to catch to take to their nest and eat.

"Time of Dinoshi, time of fear," is what they said.

The people were all living in fear because of those birds. They hid in caves, in bushes. They watched out of the corners of their eyes. They didn't dare go out.

Now some of the hidden men made bows and arrows and spears.

"Let's go out and kill them," they said.

They shot their arrows. They threw their spears. Nothing. They just bounced off the Dinoshi's armor. No one could kill them. The Dinoshi kept catching them. They ate men, women, children, everyone.

There was a wise man. His name was Kudene. He was like an anaconda. He mixed up some thick, black stuff called *curare* and put it in a pot to cook. It was the first *curare.* He made it to kill the Dinoshi.

Kudene gave it to Iahi, the trumpeter. Then Iahi went to Kudi huha and hid so he could watch the Dinoshi.

When he returned, he said: "I saw them. Now I know how to kill them. They don't have any armor on their backs. I can shoot them on their backs."

Now he prepared an arrow with *curare.* Kudene sent him back again to shoot it. When he went there, he got up above and shot the Dinoshi in their backs.

When the arrows landed, they started screaming. They took off and flew around and around. Then they began falling, spinning in circles, dropping their feathers. When the feathers landed, they began to sprout. They turned into *kurata*.

First the feathers fell over the Merevari. Then they fell over the Antawari. Now good blowgun cane grows wild over there.

Now the Dinoshi were falling. They were dying, coming down right over Marahuaka. They circled over its three peaks, T'damadu, Tahashiho, Tonoro hidi.

Then they fell on Tahashiho. Their bones stuck in the ground there. The biggest and straightest blowgun cane grows there now.

The feathers, the Dinoshi bones, only fell on our lands. That's why only we have blowguns. We own them. When other people want blowguns, they come walking. They come walking to ask us for *kurata*. They bring us things of theirs to trade with. The old people didn't have blowguns in the beginning. They found out about *curare* and blowguns when the Dinoshi died. The Marahuaka peak called Tahashiho is the blowgun mountain. No one but us knows the way. It's our mountain. It has lots of tall, straight blowgun cane.

When the Dinoshi fell, Kahuakadi was living in Tahashiho. That man said: "Good. The cane is mine now. I'm the blowgun master."

Now when we go to collect it there, when we come to that peak of Marahuaka, we ask permission from its master, Kahuakadi. We come and we say to him: "We're here to ask you for blowgun cane. We haven't eaten. We haven't touched our women." As we come up the blowgun path, we play our flutes. We plant our shoots in the earth when we get there, as offerings to Kahuakadi. We sing softly. We don't shout. We ask quietly so the master doesn't get angry. We never cut more than four canes together. That way we don't upset the master. That way we get *kurata* to make blowguns.

That was all in the beginning. Okay.

WACHAMADI

That woman kept on taking yuca from her brother's *conuco*. He didn't want that, so he said: "I'm going to punish her."

In the beginning, there weren't any snakes on the Earth. The snakes were all powerful people then who lived in the Sky. Ñomo was their mistress, their mother. She was a beautiful woman, but very evil.

Kasenadu went to Ñomo's house. He asked her for guards for his *conuco*. He wanted to catch his sister.

"Good," said Ñomo. She gave him four of her children to guard his *conuco*.

When they came to Earth, they turned into poisonous snakes. Their names were Enneku, Sede'detiu, Könnötö, and T'dadema. They were the first poisonous snakes.*

Now Kasenadu put them in the corners of his *conuco*. They hid there in the brush. Then they heard steps. They picked up their heads. They stuck out their tongues.

Now that girl came into the *conuco*. As she came in, the four guards all jumped out at once and bit her. They filled her with poison. Then they went to tell Kasenadu.

When her brother arrived, the girl said: "I have a fever, like fire burning inside me. Help me. Give me some *iukuta*. I'm dying of thirst."

That man didn't want to. He didn't do anything. He wanted his sister to die. He just looked at the woman without saying anything. He was happy.

---

*Enneku is a bushmaster, Sede'detiu a rattlesnake, Könnötö a fer-de-lance, and T'dadema a coral snake.

Now she began dreaming. Her *akato* went travelling outside her body. It went dreaming to Ñomo's house, to the mistress of that poison.

Now dreaming the woman said: "I'm thirsty. Give me something to drink."

Now Ñomo came out with a gourd in her hand: "Here, drink this *iukuta*. It'll make you better."

The woman took the gourd. It wasn't *iukuta*. It was a trick.

When she drank it, she forgot her empty body there on Earth. She stayed there dreaming, dreaming forever as a spirit in Ñomo's house. She's still a prisoner there because of the drink Ñomo gave her, when she told her: "Here. Take this *iukuta*." She never returned to her body. That's how she died. Now she's like a spirit in the Snake House. Because of that poison. Because of the wickedness of her brother, Kasenadu.

Now we remember that dead person and when anyone's bitten by snakes, right away we give them lots of *iukuta* to drink. That way they don't go off dreaming to ask for something to drink. They don't get tricked. They drink a lot and put out the poison. They don't leave their body.

When that woman died, Kasenadu cut her up. He put the pieces up on a rack.

"I'll come back later," he said. "I'll get her bones and skull."

When he cut open her stomach, two children, not born yet, fell out. They rolled down into the underbrush. They were just left there. Night came. Day came. Then another and another and a lot more. The bones were clean now. The man came back to get them. He found the two boys there, the sons of that cut up woman. The older one was named Wedame; the younger Wachamadi.

Kasenadu had two young daughters.

"Come home with me," he said. "I have two girls for you."

"Okay," said Wachamadi.

Wedame didn't say anything. He didn't want to go to that man's house. He stayed out in the jungle alone. Wachamadi went with Kasenadu to meet the girls.

When day came, Kasenadu told him: "Okay. I'm going hunting. I'll be back before nightfall. You're going to make a new *conuco* and a new house. Then I want you to weave some *sebucans*."

He took him to an enormous, overgrown hill. There were trees all around there; huge, thick ones with lots of vines, all thorny and tangled up. "Cut it all down. Clear the whole thing. Then burn it. This will be the new *conuco*. Have it ready by tonight."

He took him to another hill. "Put the new house here. Have it ready by tonight."

Then he took him to a clearing. There was a huge pile of bark there. "You'll weave this bark. I want lots of *sebucans* for the festivals, for the new house and the new *conuco*. Have everything ready by tonight."

"Okay," Wachamadi said.

Kasenadu went hunting. Now that boy thought: "How can I do all this?"

He sat down on a rock, elbows on his knees, head in his hands. He didn't eat. He didn't speak. He just thought: "How can I do it?" He just sat there, thinking and thinking.

Now the sun was getting higher and higher. It was straight up in the sky now. The boy didn't move. He just sat there thinking.

As he was thinking, Kuinadi suddenly appeared from a *moriche* palm. He was a beautiful bird, old and wise. He was the master of the *moriche*.

"Here's how you'll do it," said the bird.

Now that boy watched the bird, happy. Kuinadi picked up a palm leaf. He burned it and stuck the ashes in a gourd full of *iukuta*.

"Drink!" he said. And he gave the boy the gourd.

He drank it. Right away he felt the power of the *moriche* ashes. He felt the strength of four hundred arms in his arm. He picked up the axe and started to cut. It was as if he wasn't working at all. He didn't get tired. He just went on cutting and cutting. The axe seemed to be doing all the work by itself.

We haven't forgotten what Kuinadi showed us. When we go out to work, we always ask for his power, for those *moriche* ashes.

Wachamadi's axe chopped down trees large and small. It cut down vines and scattered thorns and thickets. The whole forest came down. Wachamadi was happy. He wasn't tired.

Then he burned it. He cleared the *conuco*. Then he said: "It's done."

Now he went to the other hill. He cleared the whole thing and built the new house.

Then he went to the clearing with the bark. He took the pile of bark and turned it into a pile of *sebucans*.

The sun was still high in the sky.

Now the boy said: "It's all done." He sat down by the foot of the *moriche*. Now he dreamed. He heard Kuinadi's voice as he dreamed: "Why are you working so hard for that man? He doesn't want you. He's a bad man. He killed your mother and your brothers. Now he's going to kill you."

"Okay," Wachamadi dreamed. "I'll kill him first. Now I'll avenge my mother, my brothers."

Then he heard Thunder. He saw Lightning in the clouds. It slid along like a snake on fire. Dreaming, he heard Kasenadu hunting.

"I'll discover his secret. I'll find out what it is. How will I do it?"

He was thinking, sitting at the foot of that *moriche*.

As he was thinking, Tukui, the hummingbird, flew up.

"I know the way," he said.

He was fast and very small. He could go anywhere and no one could see him. He knew Lightning's path.

"Okay," said that boy. "Help me then. Go and watch. Discover the secret and come back and tell me."

"Okay," said Tukui. He went and watched. Then he came back and told him. "I discovered it," he said. "I saw Lightning."

"What is it?" Wachamadi asked.

"A cane explodes and Lightning jumps out. That's how that man hunts. He shoots everything he finds. Arakusa, that's what they call his cane."

"Good," said Wachamadi. "Now I know. I'll steal it. I'll make a fake Arakusa and then I'll switch them."

Now he said: "Go look. Make a drawing of Arakusa."

"Okay," said Tukui. And he flew off.

"How will I do it?" he thought. He didn't know how to draw. Along the way, he met Matuto, the butterfly.

Matuto spent all his time painting pictures on his wings. Every day he painted them with different pictures. He sucked flowers with his long nose. He went around gathering powders and oils and then he painted his wings with them.

"Help me," Tukui said. "I have to draw something and I don't know how."

"Okay," said Matuto. He went and saw Arakusa. He drew a beautiful picture of it on his wings.

Then Tukui and Matuto took it back. The boy looked at it on Butterfly's wings. Now he knew. He got a cane. He carved it. He gave it Arakusa's body. When he carved it, he made an Arakusa. It was just like the other. It didn't have any power, just the form. It was just a fake.

"It's done," he said to Hummingbird. "Quick, take it. Go switch it with the good one."

Kasenadu was loading peccary into his basket when Tukui flew up. He wasn't watching Arakusa. It was leaning up against a tree. Tukui rushed up. He switched them without a sound. Kasenadu didn't see him. He didn't know. He was fooled.

Now he didn't have any power. Wachamadi robbed it to punish him for his evilness. That's when the people's fear ended.

Now night came and Kasenadu returned. He had the fake Arakusa hidden.

Wachamadi was asleep under the *moriche* palm when he came back. He gave him a kick.

"Did you finish your work?" he asked.

The boy sat up. He yawned. He didn't answer.

"Lazy good-for-nothing!" the man shouted. "Did you finish the *conuco*? The house? The *sebucans*?"

"I was dreaming I was cutting, chopping down trees, building houses, weaving *sebucans*."

"Dreaming!" screamed the man. "Now we'll see!" Kasenadu thought: "Good. He didn't do anything. Now I can kill him."

He went to the hill. There weren't any trees there. The new *conuco* was there. That man was amazed. "How'd he do it?" he thought. "Where'd he get that much power?" He didn't say anything. He just thought it.

Now he went to look at the other hill. The new house was there. It was right in front of him! Now the *sebucans*. They were there too!

"Okay," thought Kasenadu. "That boy's a *huhai*. His power's dangerous. I'm going to kill him."

"Okay," he said to the boy. "You finished your work. Now you're my son-in-law. We'll celebrate. I'll call the people to dance. Now we'll drink and sing."

Right away he called: "Come tomorrow. I have a new *conuco*. A new house."

Women came from all over to grate yuca. They filled a *kanawa* with *iarake*. The men came too to braid palm skirts and dance hats. Musicians came with bamboo horns. Within three days, everything was ready. They started singing. The women brought out gourds filled with *iarake*. The new house was very large, very beautiful. It had big posts and beams. Now Kasenadu's old house looked run-down and miserable. It was a sign of Wachamadi's power. Lightning Man, Kasenadu, he didn't know. He was thinking: "We'll drink. When that boy's drunk, I'll kill him."

"Let's see who can drink the most," he said.

Wachamadi drank one gourdful after another. Each time, he went out of the house and spit it out. Then he came back in and drank another. That's how he fooled Kasenadu. He didn't get drunk.

Kasenadu thought: "He's drunk. Now's the time to kill him." He went to get Arakusa, hidden behind the door. He aimed at the boy. Someone saw him and screamed: "Watch out, boy! That old man's going to kill you with that cane!"

Wachamadi didn't move. He wasn't afraid. He was laughing. Then he said: "That cane is Arakusa, the arquebus, Lightning. Now you know the secret. That's his power."

The house was filled with people. Kasenadu tried to shoot. Nothing. Arakusa was silent, dead. It had no Lightning, no Thunder. Everyone was looking at that fake. They couldn't see any power. It didn't do anything. At first the man was surprised. Then he got furious. He just pointed it and that boy rolled over laughing. Now the people started to. They weren't afraid anymore. First one broke out laughing, then another and another until everyone was laughing. They didn't like that old Lightning Man. They were just afraid of him. That's why they were so happy.

As they were laughing, Thunder came. Lightning came like a snake on fire. It didn't come out of Kasenadu's hands. It came the other way. He fell down. There was nothing left but ashes. Then the people looked over at that boy. He had his own Arakusa. It was the good one. It had power. Lightning jumped out. It struck Kasenadu.

Then they ran out screaming. They were frightened and drunk. They were falling all over each other.

That man's daughter was crying, blowing on the ashes, saying: "Not dead, drunk. Not dead, drunk."

Now Kasenadu rose from the ashes with a new body. Lightning couldn't kill him. There he was again. The girl blew on him. She was happy.

"Okay," said Wachamadi. "This isn't your house anymore. It's mine. Lightning's mine, not yours."

Then he said to him: "I'm going hunting. You're going to make a new *conuco*. I'll be back before night.".

He took him into the jungle and showed him a spot with huge, thick trees all around.

"I can't do it all alone," said Kasenadu. "I don't have that much power. If you help me, all right."

"Okay. I'll help you," said Wachamadi.

He called the yellowtails and the peccaries to cut the trees.

"Leave just one. That tall, thick one there. Kasenadu will cut that one."

The yellowtails and the peccary cut the small ones. They didn't knock them down though.

Wachamadi said: "Okay. It's done. Now that man can cut his big tree. When it falls, the small ones will fall too."

That's the way Wachamadi taught us to clear *conucos*.

Now Kasenadu hit the big tree with his axe. The axe just bounced off the hard wood. Nothing. He couldn't cut it.

Then Wachamadi said: "Okay. It's time. Everything's down now. I'm going to burn it."

Nothing was down. That man was still chopping. Wachamadi knew that. He just wanted to kill him, as punishment, as a message.

He set the brush on fire. The fire spread all around with Kasenadu in the middle.

The fire and smoke were everywhere. He couldn't escape. The one who had Thunder first was killed. Because of him, the people had been afraid. Now they knew what Thunder and Lightning were. Their new master was good.

That's the way the old ones tell it, the way I heard it.

Okay. That's all.

A Makiritare shaman seated on his jaguar bench.

Photographs by Barabara Brändli.

Weaving sebucans *to be used in the preparation of* cassava.

Preparing for the Adahe ademi hidi *festival, a*
Makiritare man puts on ahötte *and* womo
ansai *with the help of his wife.*

Drinking fermented iarake.

Dressed in wasai iaddi *dance skirts and playing* wanna
*horns, Makiritare men follow the lead of the dance
master who beats the* wasaha *staff.*

Listening to the Ademi edamo *sing,* So'to *dance during the* Wanwanna *with* wemue *crowns upon their heads.*

A Makiritare woman dressed for the Wanwanna.

Fishing with bow and arrow.

MOMIÑARU

═══

MOMIÑARU

There was a boy who went to live in the house of an old man. He wanted to marry the old man's daughter.

That boy was named Momiñaru. Adichawo was the name of the girl, Sahatuma the name of her father. That old man was evil. He ate human flesh.

Now dawn came and he said to the boy: "Go to the river and get my *toroha* (fish trap). Last night I dreamed it was full."

"Okay," said Momiñaru, and he went.

Now that man dreamed: "This boy comes to the river. He finds the *toroha*. He falls in the *toroha*. He tries to get out. He can't. He's trapped."

As that man dreamed, the boy came to the river. He fell in the *toroha*. The man was in his house, asleep in his hammock, just dreaming.

Now he dreamed: "There's a jaguar. He's walking toward the river. He sees the *toroha*. He thinks: 'Good. Here's my dinner.' He opens the *toroha*. Now he's going to eat the boy."

As the old man was dreaming in his hammock, a jaguar came down to the river. He opened the *toroha* to eat the boy.

Now the jaguar was that same Sahatuma. He was that man's dream: Sahatuma in his hammock, quietly sleeping, the jaguar in the river, like a spirit, like a dream.

When he saw him, the boy became afraid. He thought: "This jaguar's a trick. It's Sahatuma coming to eat me." He tried to get out of the trap. He couldn't. The jaguar opened the *toroha*, laughing.

Now the boy turns into a crab. The jaguar catches him. The crab bites him. The jaguar lets go. The crab gets away. The jaguar chases him.

Now Saroro, the otter, comes by and sees the crab. "There goes my dinner," he says, and he starts to chase him. He swallows the crab and runs off. And so the jaguar was outsmarted.

When that old man woke up in his hammock, the dream was over and the jaguar disappeared.

Adichawo said to her father: "The boy hasn't returned from the river. Go see what happened."

Sahatuma said: "He's not coming back. I dreamed he fell in the trap. He didn't know how to fish. When he fell in, he drowned. That boy wasn't any good. You'll find another husband now."

On the river bank, that Otter thought: "It's getting late. It's time to head back to my cave." Before he got in the cave, he went in the woods. That's what he always did. He never got his cave dirty. Now that crab came out. He was free. It was Momiñaru, the boy. He was really sick. He was half dead from suffocation when he came out of Saroro's stomach. To keep from dying, he went up to the Sky, to Aku-enaña. He dove into Lake Akuena. Then he came out brand new and healthy again with another body. He looked like another boy when he came out of that lake. It was the same Momiñaru but with another body.

Now he thought: "I'll go back to Earth. I'm going to punish that old man."

Sahatuma was up in a *madi* tree, collecting fruit in a basket with his daughter. That boy came up to the foot of the tree.

As he came up, he thought: "Fruit's falling." Some fruit was dropping. It was falling out of the basket and rolling on the ground.

The girl, Adichawo, jumped out of the tree and ran after the fruit. Now she saw the boy. She didn't recognize him. She didn't know who he was. He had a new body.

"I'm here," he said.

"Who are you?" the girl asked. "What are you doing here?"

"My name is Kaichama," said Momiñaru. "I came from over there. I want to get married."

Adichawo looked at him. He was strong and handsome. She thought: "This'll be my new husband. The first one died in the *to-roha*."

She called her father: "A boy is here. A son-in-law."

"Good," said Sahatuma. He was up in the tree eating *madi* fruit.

Now Kaichama went to the house in his disguise. It was the same Momiñaru. They didn't know that.

Now dawn came and that old man said: "I'm hungry. Yesterday I put out a trap for paca. Last night I dreamed it was full of paca. They had all fallen in the trap. Go get them."

The boy left. Along the way he came to the ants' village. It was covered with ants everywhere. There were millions of them all over the ground. They were cutting the leaves, catching big and little animals alike. They ate everything in their path.

The boy was surrounded by ants. He ran to the river and jumped in the water. That's how he got away.

Now he went back to the house and he said to the man: "I came back to tell you I found lots of peccary along the way."

"Where are they?" he asked. "I want to catch them."

"Over there," the boy said. "You're going to kill lots of peccary."

It was a trick. It wasn't the way to the peccary, but to the ants.

When Sahatuma got there, there was nothing but ants. They crawled all over him. They cut him up and carried the pieces away on their heads. And so Sahatuma was killed as punishment.

He didn't really die though. He couldn't die. He had too much power. The ants just ate the body of that man. When they killed him, the blood spilled. A drop of blood fell down. It turned into Jaguar. It was Mado, the first Jaguar. When Sahatuma died, Jaguar's body appeared. It was the beginning of the Jaguars.

That's it.

KUAMACHI

MADO

Okay. Now let's tell the story of Kuamachi, the Evening Star. In the beginning, he was a boy. He lived on the Earth. This is the way the old ones tell it.

There was an old man. He lived with his wife and daughter. The daughter was pregnant.

One morning, the girl went out alone to gather fruit in the *conuco*. Along the way she met some people with bows and arrows. When they saw her, they shot her. They cut her up and ate her. Mado, the jaguar, was their chief. Anteater and Sosowi, the oriole, were with him. So was Lizard. There were lots of other men there with him too. They were called Shiriche, the Star People. They all killed and ate the woman together.

When they cut open her stomach, an unborn child fell out. The child rolled out and fell in the river.

When he fell in, Dihuku, the sardine, swallowed him. The unborn child grew in Dihuku's stomach. Then he came out. Now Iawa, the bass, swallowed him. He went on growing in Iawa's stomach. Then he came out. Now Namaru, the skate, came up and swallowed him. He got bigger and bigger there, waiting to be born.

Now he said: "I'm hungry. I haven't eaten. I'm going to find some food. I'll be back soon."

He was really tiny when he came out. He jumped up on the bank. He went into the jungle. He came to a *conuco* full of sweet peppers.

"Good," he said. "Here's my food."

He stuffed himself. Then he went back to Namaru's stomach.

Now the owner of that *conuco* came to get some peppers. There were hardly any left. "Someone's robbed me," he thought. "I'm going to get a guard."

He called Kadau, the caracara: "Watch this *conuco*. If anyone comes to rob it, call me."

The next day, that boy from the river was hungry again. "I'm going out," he said. "I'm going back to that *conuco*."

He came out of Namaru and went off. He went back to the *conuco* and took some peppers. Kadau started singing. The owner of the *conuco* came running up. He hit the boy. He took him for the thief.

That man's name was Mahanama. He was Kuamachi's grandfather.

"Why'd you hit me?" asked the boy. "I'm so little."

"You weren't stealing my peppers?" said the old man.

"You're not my grandfather?" answered the boy.

Mahanama didn't know. He didn't recognize that boy. Now he was really happy. He knew who he was. "You can eat all you want," he told him. "This is your *conuco*. This is your home." The boy ate. He gorged himself. Now he stayed in his grandfather's house. He went on growing. He became a man.

The grandfather said: "I'm old. I can't fight. You'll have to avenge your mother."

"I'll avenge her death," the young man said. "I'll go find the ones who did it."

Along the way, he came to a house. Waremo, the anteater, lived there. He had killed the boy's mother. He stopped in front of his house. He heard music. There was a festival going on. Lots of people were inside, dancing and drinking.

"I'm here," said Kuamachi. "I was just out hunting, passing by."

"You're here," said Waremo. "Okay."

"Tell me. When you want to kill people, where do you hit them?" he asked.

"There!" Waremo answered, pointing to his neck and shoulders.

"Ahh," said the boy and he rubbed his hand over Waremo's neck and shoulders. His hand had soot on it. That's how Anteater got his marks. He's still that way, with marks, today.

Waremo looked at that stranger suspiciously. "What?" he thought. "Why'd he mark me?"

Then he said: "There's another way to kill. Come inside and I'll show you."

He made the boy come in. The house was packed. Waremo let out a big, smelly fart. The stench was unbearable. You couldn't breathe. People were gagging, falling all over. They were looking for the door, screaming like madmen. That's what Anteater still does when he's mad.

Waremo was laughing. "You see?" he said. "That's how I kill." And he went out.

The boy followed him. He chased him with a club. He hit him on the neck, on his shoulders. He beat him on the marks. He killed him.

"That's a way to kill too," he said.

He started along the Star People's path again.

A little ways on, there was a stream. Iaruruko, the lizard, came by paddling a canoe. That man was bad. He had eaten the boy's mother too.

"What are you doing here?" he asked.

"Hunting, looking around," said the boy.

"Okay. I'm canoeing, fishing."

"Tell me. When you kill people, how do you hide the body?"

Iaruruko looked at him suspiciously. "Look. Here's how I do it." And he jumped out of the canoe and turned into a lizard and disappeared.

The boy jumped in behind him, turning over stones, looking all over the bottom of that stream for him. He couldn't find him.

He was still looking when night came. Now another canoe passed by with another man in it.

"What are you looking for under those rocks?" he asked.

"Iaruruko got away from me. I want to find him and kill him."

"You won't find him in the stream," the man answered, laughing.

"Where is he?" he asked.

"I'm Iaruruko," and like a lizard, he slid into the water and got away again.

Now night came. The boy couldn't see anymore. "Okay," he said. "That Lizard has power. I'll catch him another day."

Now he followed Mado's path. When he left, the grandfather gave him a trap and a bundle of sticks.

A beautiful girl came up along the path. "I like you," said Kuamachi. "Who's your father? Where's your house?"

"Okay," answered the girl. "My father's Mado, the jaguar. My house is that cave behind the mountain."

"Let's go," said the boy.

"Okay," said the girl.

The two of them went off.

As they were coming up, Kuamachi said: "Wait for me. I want to look over there. I'll be right back." The girl waited on the path. The boy hid his trap and sticks in a bush. Then he came back. "Let's go," he said.

"Let's go," she answered.

When they got there, she called her father. "I'm here," she said. "I met this boy along the way. I've brought you a son-in-law."

"Good," said Mado. "You brought my dinner."

"Not your dinner," she answered. "Your son-in-law."

"Okay," said Mado.

Now Kuamachi began to work for him.

When the sun rose, Jaguar told the boy: "I'm going hunting. I'll be back later."

The boy said: "I dreamed, I was in a cave. There was water. I saw my reflection in the water. That's what I dreamed."

"Good," answered Mado. "That's a good dream, a good sign. You're going to catch pacas." And he gave him a trap to use.

Kuamachi picked up the trap. It wasn't any good. It was a trick, too big for pacas. It was old and broken, completely useless.

Now Mado spoke to the girl in a whisper. He thought Kuamachi couldn't hear him. Kuamachi was listening through the wall.

"You brought that boy to eat," he said. "I'm going to the other cave now. I'll wait for you there to kill him. Say to him: 'Let's hunt paca. I'll take you. I know the caves.' That's how you'll get him to the other cave."

"He's not to eat," the girl answered. "He's my husband."

"I'll wait for you in the other cave," said Mado. Then he turned into a jaguar and went off. The boy knew now. He heard everything.

The girl came over to Kuamachi's hammock. She was carrying a gourd filled with *onoto* and oil and a brush to paint with.

"Let's hunt paca," she said to him. "Here, I'll paint you." She began covering him with good paca drawings. She painted his face, his chest, his arms, his legs, everything.

"Make me beautiful," Kuamachi said. He stayed still so she could paint him.

Now the girl was painting him, looking at his face. "What a pity," she thought. "He's such a good husband." She didn't say anything. She just thought it. She hid the truth. She was afraid to say anything.

Now she was crying, trying to hide the tears. Now a tear rolled down on Kuamachi's chest.

"What's that?" he asked.

"Sweat," she answered. "I'm sweating."

It was a lie. She was thinking about the boy's death, that's why she was crying. She didn't tell him the truth. Kuamachi knew that she was crying, that she was lying. He just looked at her. He didn't say anything.

"It's done," she said. "You're all painted. Let's go hunting now." Kuamachi picked up the trap. The girl led.

"The hiding places are over there," she said.

"Okay," Kuamachi answered. "Wait for me. I'm going to look. I'll be right back."

She waited for him on the path. He went to the bush where the trap and sticks were hidden. He switched the bad trap with the good one. He picked up the sticks. He threw away the bad one.

As he switched the traps, he thought: "I'm going to fool Jaguar. Now I'm going to catch him."

He went back to the path. "Let's go," he said.

"Let's go," the girl answered.

She showed him where the pacas were. Kuamachi looked in the cave. There weren't any pacas in there. It was a trick. The woman was pretending. She didn't know. Kuamachi didn't say anything. They started walking again.

Now she said: "This is the cave. It has two mouths. I'll stand at this mouth and scare the pacas. You set the trap up at the other mouth; then call me. Shout: 'I'm ready.'" That's what the woman said.

Kuamachi went to the other mouth with the trap. The woman was waiting for the signal, the boy's call. He didn't call. He didn't say anything.

"Are you ready?" she screamed. The boy wasn't answering.

"Can't you hear?" she called.

Now he answered: "Okay, it's ready."

"Okay," she answered. "I'm going to scare the pacas now. They're going to come out that mouth."

She stuck a branch in the hole. She shook it. There weren't any pacas. It was a trick. It was a signal for Jaguar. He was in the cave. He leapt out into the trap. He was rolling over and over, howling and screaming, mad as could be. He couldn't get out. The trap was a good one. He couldn't get out and he couldn't eat Kuamachi the way he'd wanted to. And that's how the boy beat him.

Now Kuamachi came up with the sticks. Jaguar was crying and

begging, jumping all over the trap. Now the girl got in the trap with him.

"Don't kill him!" she screamed. "Have mercy. He's my father." Kuamachi didn't listen. He took his revenge. He killed Jaguar to avenge his mother, and Jaguar's daughter because she lied. He did it as a sign of justice.

Now he went to look for his mother's skull. Jaguar's house was filled with skulls. They were hanging from all over like trophies. Kuamachi looked at one, then another and another. He looked at all of them. He couldn't recognize his mother's.

An old man came in.

"What are you doing here?" he said. "This is our house, the jaguars'."

Kuamachi didn't answer. He killed the old man. He went on looking through the skulls.

"What are you doing here?" said another one. "What do you want, a skull?"

This one was a jaguar child.

"I'm looking for my mother's," he answered. "I'm Kuamachi. Your father ate my mother."

"I know the names of the skulls," the child said.

Now he gave him the skull. Kuamachi took it. Mahanama really celebrated when his grandson came back, blowing the skull like a trumpet. "Uuuuu . . . uuuuu," sounded the skull when that boy got back to his grandfather's house.

WLAHA

Okay. In the beginning, the night sky was empty, black. The Stars were people. They lived on the Earth. They had their village at the foot of Kushamakari. It was full of powerful people. Their old ones knew a lot. One day, they all went out to hunt with Jaguar. They listened to that Jaguar. That's why they killed and ate a woman. As punishment, they were chased. That's why they fled up into the bad sky, the sky of this Earth.

Now we'll tell the story of the Stars.

Dawn came and Kuamachi followed the path toward Shiricheña, the village of those people called Stars.

As he came up to it, he sat down on the edge of the path and thought: "There are a lot of them and powerful. How will I kill them?"

He had some *dewaka* fruit in a basket. "Okay," he thought now. "I'll invite them to collect *dewaka*." He got up and went into Shiricheña. Wlaha was the chief of the village.

"Here I am," said the boy.

"Where'd you come from?" asked Wlaha. "What are you doing here?"

"I've come from my grandfather, Mahanama's house. Our trees are full of *dewaka* fruit. There are just the two of us. I've come to ask for help. We need people to harvest them. Then we'll divide it."

"I'll ask," said Wlaha. "Wait here for my answer."

He gathered the elders. "A boy has come, the grandson of Mahanama. He says they have a harvest. He's asking for our help."

They deliberated. First one talked, then another. Then they said: "We don't trust Mahanama. We killed his daughter. We better stay here."

Wlaha called Kuamachi. "We can't," he told him.

"Too bad," said that boy, chewing on a *dewaka*. "They're good and there are plenty of them. All we have to do is pick them. Want to try one?" And he gave him a *dewaka*.

Wlaha tasted it. "Mmmmm. That is good," he said. "But we don't want to."

"Okay," Kuamachi said. "I'm going. Here's some more for your people to try."

"Okay," said Wlaha and he took the fruit. He called the people. They tried them. "Delicious," said one.

"I really like them," said another and another and another. Then they discussed it again, everyone talking. Kuamachi was waiting. He wasn't leaving.

When Wlaha came back, the boy said: "Okay. I'm going." He was just saying that. He wasn't going.

"Wait," he said. "Where are the *dewaka?*"

"Over there. There are lots of them in those woods."

"Okay," he answered. "We'll go with you."

"Good. Let's go."

They left, walking through the jungle, going up and over the hills and mountains.

Kuamachi said: "Wait. I'm going to get my grandfather. He knows the way. I'll be right back."

He came back with the old man. Then Mahanama led the way. And so they got there.

The Stars climbed right up in the trees. They didn't wait for anyone to tell them. They just climbed up and started eating.

"Okay," said Mahanama. "I'm going to weave baskets for the harvest."

When they heard that, they broke out laughing. They were just eating. There were lots of them. There were just two of the other ones. That's why they forgot about them. They didn't want to gather anything. They just ate like Jaguar and Tapir at Marahuaka.

"Okay," thought Kuamachi. "The food doesn't matter to me. It's only a trick to kill them."

"I'm going to go up and gather," he said.

"I'll stay down here and weave the baskets," said the grandfather.

Kuamachi climbed up a tree. He picked a fruit. He dropped it down. When the fruit fell, water came out. It spread. It flooded the forest.

Kuamachi thought: "Canoe." There was a canoe. "Jump, grandfather," he called. Mahanama jumped into the canoe with his baskets. You couldn't see the Earth anymore, just trees and water.

Now Mahanama stacked a pile of baskets up in the canoe. He started throwing them in the water. He threw in one. It turned into an anaconda. Another, a crocodile. Another, a caiman. Another, a piranha. Another, a stingray. The water was filled with deadly animals and *mawadi*. Mahanama was weaving as fast as he could, throwing out baskets.

Those men were up above, watching. They were frightened.

Wlaha thought: "What'll we do? If we go down, the animals will eat us. We can't escape." Now he was afraid.

"What are you throwing those baskets away for?" he called to the old man. "We're up here collecting to fill them. We're working as partners."

When they heard that, the grandfather and the boy burst out laughing. That man was talking out of fear. It wasn't true. He wasn't laughing now.

Kuamachi found a nest of white ants in the tree. He set it on fire. Now the whole forest filled up with smoke. The boy jumped into the canoe and started paddling. He went off with his grandfather.

"Let's get bows and arrows and kill them." They paddled off to find them. There was water everywhere. Now they found the bows and arrows the boy had hidden in a cave.

When they went back into the forest, they couldn't see anything, just smoke all above the water. They could hear the people up in the trees coughing and choking from the smoke.

When the smoke cleared, they saw them all hanging on there in the trees. They were crying, begging for mercy. They weren't eating now.

Kuamachi stood up in the canoe and pointed his bow at Wlaha.

"No!" he screamed. "Hold your arrow. We're going to work now."

When the boy shot the arrow, Wlaha hid in the branches. Kuamachi shot another. A man dropped in the water. The animals devoured him. Now another and another. He shot. They fell. He shot. They fell. The animals were coming up, looking for food. Caimans, anacondas, legs, heads, they were all floating and tossing around together. Everything was red with the Stars' blood. The *mawadi* were swallowing them with one bite. The arrows were falling like rain. You just heard "w'lok," and a body would fall. And then "d'lek," the snapping of the caimans' jaws.

"Okay, give me another arrow," Kuamachi said to his grandfather.

"They're all gone," he answered.

The sun was setting. There were seven men left in the trees. The rest had fallen to the caimans. Others were swimming around wounded, screaming, trying to escape.

The seven men were Wlaha. That man had been left alone in the trees. Now he turned into seven. He didn't want to give up.

Now Mahanama was paddling the canoe, circling around in the water. Kuamachi was looking for arrows. Nothing. Only animals and pieces of flesh floating around.

"Where'd my arrows fall?"

"Here they are!" shouted Wlaha. He was up in the trees laughing. Kuamachi looked at the seven Wlaha. They were clutching seven arrows. Now they were going to shoot.

The arrows never fell. Wlaha had caught them as they landed. He was racing all around as the boy was shooting.

Now Kuamachi didn't have any. Seven men were watching him, clutching arrows, laughing.

He hid in the bottom of the canoe with his grandfather.

Wlaha called to his men. Many were dead. Others were still alive, hidden in the water.

First a man came out of the water dripping with blood. He was carrying his leg in his hands. He was saying: "They just cut off my leg. They didn't eat it. I still have it." He grabbed onto the tree. He climbed up the best he could. And so he got away. They called him Ihette, One Leg.

Now the Stars were fleeing from the *mawadi* and the other animals. Another man got out, then another and another, lots of them. They climbed up and gathered in the trees again. They weren't talking.

Wlaha was calling them. They were coming. They were gnawed, gored, half dead with fear. They were just thinking about getting away.

Wlaha was standing up in the tree. He had taken his seven *damodede,* his seven Wlaha, out of his body. They were looking up at the black sky, clutching their seven arrows, each one his own. Now they aimed at the sky. It was night now.

Wlaha told them: "Okay. You're here. You're safe. All of us still alive are together. Now we have the arrows. We're going to shoot them. We're sick and wounded. We're going to go far away from this hell-hole. We're going to leave this Earth."

"Let's go," they answered.

"Now we'll shoot the arrows and make a ladder. We'll go to Heaven. Who wants to go first? Who'll tie the rungs together?"

Everyone was silent.

There was a man in front of Wlaha. He was just listening, looking at the arrows. He was shaking, still thinking about the water and the caimans. He was scared. He didn't say anything.

"Okay. You!" said Wlaha looking at him. "I'll shoot the arrow. You go flying after it."

"No. Not me," he said. "I can't. I can't. I'll fall."

"You're going to fly. I'm going to shoot." And he turned him into a bird.

The bird shook. His voice trembled. "Watte! Watte! I'm going to fall. I'm going to fall," he said with his eyes half shut.

"Okay. You're a coward, a frightened bird. You can stay here with the animals. From now on they'll call you Watte. Your name will be 'I can't, I'll fall.' Your grandchildren will sing just like you. They'll just say, 'Watte, watte,' and spend all their time shaking and hiding. But we're going to Heaven. Okay. Who'll go? Who'll be first? Who's going with the arrows?"

There was another man named Ahishama. He was very wise.

"Can you?" Wlaha asked.

"I'll go," Ahishama answered.

"You won't fall?"

"I'll go."

He turned him into a bird. He was beautiful, brilliant, with orange-colored feathers, and very fast and light. His name was Ahishama, the troupial.

There was another man.

"Can you?"

"I'll go."

He turned him into a frog. He was beautiful, dark blue-green. He had enormous feet and a little body. His feet stretched like a bow. His body jumped like an arrow. They called him Kütto. That's what they call his grandchildren, the frogs that still hop around today.

Wlaha shot. The arrow sped out. It flew up. Troupial flew up. Frog leapt.

Wlaha screamed: "Fly! Jump! Catch it! Tie it!"

Ahishama was carrying the end of a vine in his beak. We call that vine he had *sahudiwa,* vine-chain. It's a long, long vine, all wrinkled and creased. Frog had a little gourd of *peraman* in his mouth.

The three went up together. Ahishama caught the arrow. He tied it down with *sahudiwa.* Frog, he glued it with *peraman.*

The seven Wlaha shot another arrow and then another and another. Seven arrows in all. They hung there in space, seven rungs tied to that big vine. It was the ladder, the road to Heaven. That Troupial and that Frog built it. Ahishama and Kütto. They climbed up without a ladder. When they built it, there was no road.

They were the first ones to arrive. Right away they changed. They started shining. They were the first two stars in the black night. The very first was Ahishama, then Kütto. Now that Troupial named Ahishama burns orange (Mars). He built the ladder in space. That's what they say.

Now Wlaha leapt up; first one rung and then another and another. He climbed right up and called down to the others. "Come on!" he told them. They followed him. He was the guide for everyone.

He arrived at the top as seven men. They turned into stars, the seven *damodede,* always together (the Pleiades). Now they shine up there as a sign of union, peace, and friendship. When they hide over in one side of the sky (in May), they bring the rains. When they come out from the other side again (in July), they bring the summer, the dry time.

Wlaha's son climbed up with him too. His name is Wlaha nakomo. He turned into three stars. Mönettä, the scorpion, went up too. He turned into many stars (the Big Dipper). Then Ihette went up, slowly creeping, bleeding, carrying his cut-off leg (Orion's Belt). Now Amaduwakadi, the Morning Star, went up. He shines very bright, but only in the early morning. Others went up too: Waramidi, Warerata, the sloth, Wachedi chato, the tapir, and others, many, many others.

Kuamachi watched them as they fled up the ladder. He thought: "I'm going to go up. I want to go too."

He tried to grab the end of the vine. Ioroko was already there. He wanted to go up too. He was moving very slowly, loaded down with a basket full of poison. Kuamachi thought: "He can't go up there. He's a demon. Demons don't go to Heaven."

Then he said to him: "You're all loaded down. I'm going light. Let me get in front of you."

"Okay," said Ioroko. Kuamachi ran ahead. Now he thought: "I'll be the last. After me, no more will come." Now he called Wadakane, the crab, to cut the big vine so Ioroko would fall back down to Earth.

Crab rushed up and tried to cut the ladder. He couldn't. That vine was really strong. Crab broke his claws. Then Kuamachi called Kahshe, the piranha. He came up and cut it right away. They had just gotten there when he cut it. Ioroko was still down below, way behind; slowed down because of his load. The vine fell. The seven arrows, the rungs, went down. Ioroko fell with his poison. He sank in the water with the animals.

Wadakane, Kahshe and Kuamachi were already up. Kuamachi was the last. He had the ladder destroyed. No one else could get up after that.

When Kuamachi went up, he brought Akuaniye, the Peace Plant, with him. He gave it to Wlaha as a sign of peace, to show he'd forgotten. Because of that, he was able to come in.

"Okay," said Wlaha. "The fighting's over. We'll forget everything."

Then Kuamachi went in. Wlaha kept that Akuaniye plant as a reminder. Now he's the master of that plant. That's why the seven Wlaha always stay together, in friendship, just like one. It's a sign of peace for us.

We have Akuaniye too now. We make peace with our enemies with it. We ask and we give forgiveness. We have peace again. It was a gift from Kuamachi when all the Stars gathered together up above in the beginning and forgot their war.

Now Kuamachi said: "Good. I'm going now. I'm going to live alone, away from the others."

He found a place down below, on the horizon. He has his house there, very quiet and all alone. He just comes out at sunset. He walks around on the horizon a little bit and then he goes back in his house.

That's why they call him Kuamachi, the Evening Star.

The old ones say that the first Stars thought they had arrived in Heaven. They were looking for Heaven when they fled. But they couldn't get in. They had killed. They had eaten human flesh. Because of that, they weren't allowed in. The Scissors Master wouldn't let them pass. They never saw Kahuña's light.

They stayed further down, on this side of the door. They built their houses in the darkness, in the land of the night. They're still there now. Nuna, the moon, lives there too. That's not Heaven. We call that the night sky. It's not the real one. It's fake. Just like the one we see during the day where the sun, the rain, the birds, and the clouds travel. We can only see the things of this world. The real Sky (Heaven) is invisible. There aren't any stars there, just Wanadi, shining alone. There's no darkness, no night, no day. Just light, light and nothing else. The stars, the moon, the sun, they aren't going to live forever. They're going to fall when this Earth ends. They're going to die along with us, with Odosha. Then Wanadi will return. You'll be able to see the real Sky. Its light never goes out.

Okay, that's all.

MAKUSANI

MAKUSANI

The old ones always tell the story of a boy when he went to the house of the moon and the house of the sun. Okay. Moon and Sun are both men. Nuna, the moon, is a bad man. He eats people. Shi, the sun, is a good man.

That boy was named Makusani. He left his house and went up in the mountains to hunt. He came to a river. As he came to it, he saw a canoe. There was a beautiful girl in the canoe. He wanted to catch her. She ran away. He chased her. Then the girl turned into a frog. She hopped and hopped. Makusani ran after her.

Now the frog was far away. The boy was tired. He was way off the trail and all alone, far from the houses. He didn't know where he was. He sat down and thought: "What should I do? How am I going to get back home?"

Now another girl came. Her name is Huenna, the tinamou.

"Here I am," she said. "What are you doing here, so far from the houses?"

"I'm lost," he said. "I was chasing a frog. She got away. Now I don't know how to get back home."

"We'll go to my father's house," said the girl. She liked the boy.

The two went walking off. That house was really far. Along the way, the girl said: "I'm tired. Let's rest."

Then she said: "I'm going to sleep. Don't wake me. Don't go touching me either."

She went to sleep. The boy couldn't sleep. He wanted to touch her. Very quietly, he went up next to her. He touched her. She woke up. She turned into a tinamou and flew away. He couldn't see her anymore. He was all alone again. That's the way he was punished.

Now he was thinking: "How am I going to find my way? How am I going to get back home?"

Another canoe came by. A man was coming in it. It was Nañudi, the otter.

"I'm lost," said the boy. "I want to go home again."

"Get in," said Nañudi. "I'm going down river. I know the way."

The boy got in.

"Cover your eyes. Don't go looking at my path now."

He covered his eyes. Now he was sitting in the canoe. Nañudi was paddling. He was paddling down the river.

Now the boy wanted to look and see Nañudi's secret. He spread his fingers a little bit at a time. He opened his eyes. "I want to look," he thought. "Nañudi's not watching."

Then he looked. Nañudi saw him. He turned into an otter. He jumped into the water and disappeared. The boy was in the canoe all alone again. He didn't know where he was. That's how he was punished.

Night came. Makusani climbed up in a tree to sleep.

While he was up there, a fisherman came by with a trap and a basket full of fish. It was Nuna, the moon man.

Nuna saw the reflection of the tree in the water. He could see the boy in it.

"Good," he thought. "There's a boy living in the water. I'm going to catch him."

He put in his trap. He tried to catch the reflection. Nothing. He couldn't catch it. Makusani was watching him from above, laughing without making a sound.

Now he wanted to surprise the fisherman. He spit in the water. Nuna looked up. He saw him.

"Okay," he said. "He doesn't live in the river. He lives up in the tree, like a bird."

Then he caught him. He put him in his basket and carried him away with the fish.

When he got home to Nunaña, his daughter saw the boy. "Good," she said to her father. "You brought me a husband."

"He's not your husband," said Nuna. "I brought him to eat. Tomorrow I'll roast him. He's just to eat."

Dawn came and he told the boy: "I'm going to roast the fish. Go cut firewood."

He went off with that man's daughter. He cut lots of firewood. The girl carried the wood. They went back home.

"Okay," said Nuna. "That's not enough. Go back and cut some more. I need firewood for my food."

Makusani went out again. Now he took that man's other daughter, the younger one.

He cut. The girl gathered.

"Why so much wood?" asked Makusani. "This is a lot for fish."

"For fish, no. For you," said the girl.

"Okay," Makusani thought. "Now I understand. I'm going to get out of here."

He picked up a handful of sand. He threw it on the girl's legs, screaming: "Watch out! I've stepped on a wasps' nest! The wasps are mad!"

The girl was frightened. She screamed. She just ran and didn't look back. She ran all the way to her father's house. Now Makusani started running the other way. He didn't go back to that man's house.

As he was running, he saw a light. "There's another house," he thought. He went on running toward that light. It was really bright. It was the light from Shiña, the Sun House.

"Who are you?" the Sun asked. "Where did you come from?"

"My name is Makusani. I came from Nunaña. I ran away. Nuna wants to eat me."

"Hide," he answered. "That man's on his way here now to find you."

The boy hid in a big jar. Now Nuna came in, boiling mad.

"You haven't seen a boy, have you? I'm looking for him. He ran away from my house."

"I don't know. I haven't seen anyone," said the Sun. "Get out of here. The only reason you look for people is to eat them."

Nuna didn't pay any attention. He began looking all around. Shi didn't say anything. He just shined and got hotter and hotter and hotter. It got so hot that Nuna couldn't look anymore and went running out.

"You can come out now," said Shi to the boy. "He won't come back. He doesn't like light."

In the morning, he gave the boy a blowgun.

"Go out and catch some birds. Don't go looking through the blowgun's hole now."

Makusani went out hunting with that blowgun. He took the Sun's daughter. The two of them went walking along together.

Now he thought: "Why did he tell me not to look through the blowgun's hole? I want to look."

Then he said to the girl: "What do you see when you look through the hole in the blowgun?"

"You see the Earth," the girl said. "You see all the people and villages down there."

"Good," he said. "I want to look. I want to find my way, my house. I want to see my mother. My poor mother's all alone. I want to go back and see her."

Then he said: "What will happen if I look?"

"Nothing's going to happen," said the girl. "We can look. My father's not watching."

Now the two of them looked together. They saw the Earth, the houses, the roads, the people. They were looking for one road, one house in particular.

"There it is!" said the girl. "I see it. Can you see it?"

"Yeh! There's a woman grating yuca in the doorway. It's my mother. I want to go back."

Then the two of them fell. They went spinning and tumbling through space all the way down to the Earth, to the house of that boy's mother.

As they fell, the girl turned into a gigantic snake, a boa constrictor.

"What will my mother say if she finds this snake?" the boy thought. He hid the girl in a basket inside the house.

Then he went to find his mother. She looked at him. She didn't recognize him. He had changed. He'd been gone from home such a long time. She liked him. She threw some pebbles at him, laughing, playing, running around the way women do when they want to flirt.

"What are you doing?" he said to her. "Aren't you my mother? Aren't I your son?"

Okay, now she recognized him. She was happy when she realized he had come back.

When morning came, the boy went out to hunt. "I'm going," he said. "I'll be back. Don't go looking in that basket."

"Okay," the mother answered.

As soon as the boy left, she ran to see what he had hidden in the basket. She opened the basket. Now that big snake came out.

"Who are you? What are you doing here, hiding in my house?"

"I'm the Sun's daughter," the snake said. "I'm engaged to your son."

"You're lying," she said to her. "You're just a snake." And she beat her with a stick and threw her out of the house.

The snake went into the mountains and found Makusani.

"Your mother threw me out of the house. She beat me. I can't live there."

"Okay," he answered. "We'll both go. We'll go back to your father's house."

They went back to Shiña. That's where they stayed. They're still there. That's what they say.

Okay, now. That's all.

MARAHUAKA

KUCHI

Those old people were very poor now. They had no food. There weren't any trees on the Earth. They had no *conucos*. They ate dirt and nothing else. They sent their children out to gather it in *tudi*. They just ate dirt. There was no water.

It had been different in the beginning. Iamankave, the Yuca Mistress, the food keeper, she lived in the highest part of the Sky. She always sent a *damodede* with armfuls of cassava for them.

"Where do you come from?" they would ask.

"From far away," he'd say. And he gave them the cassava and left.

Iyako, the veinticuatro ant, used to come down to Earth all the time. He brought them water. "Where do you come from?" they would ask. He didn't answer. He just gave them the water and went on his way.

Then Odosha came. When he came, he ruined everything. He brought evil and sickness. Now that cassava man didn't come back anymore. Neither did that ant with the water. Hunger and thirst came.

One day, a man said: "I know the ant's road. I'm going to find water again."

That man was named Dariche. He turned into a swift. He flew off. He grew smaller and smaller in the clouds. He disappeared. Then he came back with the water. They say that he went to Akuenaña in the highest Sky, that he stole the water from Lake Akuena.

He brought it to the Kashishare (Casiquiare). He made a great pool there. They call it the Old Water. There was no water on the Earth before that. The Orinoco and the Ventuari didn't exist yet. There weren't any rivers.

Now there was just that water by the Casiquiare far away from here. It didn't run. It was all in one place, still. Dariche brought the Old Water. The old people went off to look for it. They walked and walked. When they got there they were tired. They didn't find anything but a smelly old pond.

Then another man said: "I know the cassava road. I'll go look for it again."

His name was Kuchi. Now we'll tell the story of that man.

"I know," he said. "I know the way."

He knew it. He was wise. "Once I dreamed I went to Iamankave's house in Heaven." That's what he said.

That man turned into Kuchi, the kinkajou. Then he went to Heaven. He left his body on Earth for the kinkajous of today. He was the first one, the grandfather of them all. Now that man went up to the Sky, climbing and climbing. He grew very small. You couldn't see him at all anymore. He arrived at Iamankave's house at the top of Heaven. He saw a huge *kanawa* full of *mañoco* hanging in the doorway. Near the house, in the garden, he saw the giant food tree surrounded by a fence. It was Iamankave's garden. Now he hid so Iamankave wouldn't see him.

A boy named Wedama came out of the house. He was Iamankave's son, Kuchi's friend.

Kuchi called him. "I came to find food," he said.

"You're here. Okay. Let's hide. Come with me." That's what the boy said.

He turned into a swallow. He flew over the fence, up to the top of the branches. Kuchi turned into a kinkajou. He jumped over the fence. He climbed up the trunk. They flew, they climbed up to the fruit. There was every kind of fruit up on that tree. It was the Yuca Mother. Each branch was different and filled with another kind of food.

As they ate, they shook up the wasps. They had their nest there. They guarded the tree. They were flying around now, screaming: "Someone's here! Someone's stealing the food!"

Now the Yuca Mistress knew. She came running out to see what was happening.

She came up there. The swallow hid. Kuchi ran. As he ran, he hid a little piece of that tree beneath his nail. He went on running. He couldn't get away. The Yuca Mistress caught him. She skinned him. Then she hung him on the fence without a skin.

"I'm going to die," Kuchi thought. He had a powerful, wise sister. She lived in the Sky Place. He called and called, asking her for help. The sister came. Her name is Iumakawa.

When she came, she said to him: "You stole the food. That's why you're hanging here without any skin. You got what you deserved."

"We're hungry on Earth. That's why I stole it," he said. "Help me. I'm going to die here without any skin."

His sister helped him. She asked the Yuca Mistress to forgive him. "He was hungry," she said. "He came from the Earth. There's no food there. He's my brother. That's why I'm asking you."

First the Mistress said: "He robbed the food. His punishment is fair." Then she said: "Okay. I'll forgive him." And she gave Iumakawa Kuchi's skin back. She healed her brother. She made him like new again. Now he jumped up. He ran. He went back down to Earth. He had a splinter of the tree hidden beneath his nail.

When he returned, he was like a man again. He sat down on his shaman's bench, without speaking, without doing anything, just thinking and nothing else. He waited until night. When night came, he pulled the splinter out from under his nail and planted it.

That was far away in Dodoima (Mount Roraima). During the night, the yuca began to sprout. You couldn't see it. When dawn came, there was a tall, tall tree with many branches and all sorts of fruit. "It's done," said Kuchi. He ate. He was happy when the dawn came. That was the beginning of our food, the Dodoima tree, when the people were hungry.

Dodoima was the first tree. Now we see it as a very tall mountain. Many wild fruits still grow there. No one plants them. They just grow as reminders.

Kamaso heard about it. That man lived in Kamaso wochi (Kamaso's Savanna). "Good," he said. "Kuchi has planted food in Dodoima. That's too far away. The people there can eat now. We don't have anything to eat but dirt. All we have are stories."

Kamaso sent a messenger to Roraima. She was a woman named Edenawadi. She walked for days and came to the East. She spoke with Kuchi. She asked for a yuca shoot to plant here. "Okay," said Kuchi. He gave her the shoot.

Then Edenawadi headed back toward the sunset. On her way, night fell. The night found her in a place called Uaiante (Auyan Tepui). When she arrived there, Edenawadi sat down. She planted the shoot. She dreamed of yuca, food, different fruits. When the sun came up, there was a shoot, just one little shoot. Three little green yuca leaves and nothing else. It didn't grow like a tree. It didn't have different fruits. That soil was no good.

Edenawadi picked up her shoot. She started walking toward the sunset again. When night came, she planted the yuca, in Kuntinama. Nothing. The next night in Metakuni. Nothing. The next night in Arahame. Nothing. Now she came to her house in Kamaso wochi. She gave the shoot to Kamaso. Many people came to see. They were shouting with joy: "Our food's arrived!" Kamaso planted it during the night. He sang and sang. When the sun came up, there was just one shoot. There wasn't any fruit. "This soil's no good," he said. They all went away, sad, like before, looking for dirt to eat.

There was Madunawe. She was a woman too. She lived in Wade's house in Truma achaka. She was kin to Wade.

When the news came, Wade shook with joy: "Kuchi, yuca, Dodoima, Kamaso, Edenawadi!" When the news came, he called the woman named Madunawe.

"We have good soil here," he said. "Let's ask for the shoot."

"Good," answered Madunawe. "We'll plant it."

It was nighttime when the woman planted the shoot in the black soil. All the fruits, palms, trees, vines, every green thing there is on the Earth today, was born in one night, when that woman planted the yuca.

When day came, the tree was tallllllll. They called it Marahuaka. The branches, the leaves, the fruits of Marahuaka covered the entire Earth. It was like a roof. Each branch was budding and sprouting and bearing fruit, turning into another and another and another, and every one with a different food. It was all the yuca. All the plants, all the fruits we know today began there. It was just one tree with many branches. It wouldn't stop sprouting. Every time it was something different.

The people came to look at Marahuaka. When they came, they were hungry. They were sick and thin. Now they shouted: "Marahuaka! Our food has come!"

Some were laughing. Others wept as the tree went on sprouting. There wasn't anything else. There was no food, no water, nothing on the Earth. That's what the old ones say. I didn't see it.

First they were happy, then sad. With empty stomachs, they opened up their arms, their mouths, their eyes. They just looked at the fruit. It was up there in the sky. "What'll we do now? How can we get it?" asked one after another with their arms and mouths and eyes open. They were really sad as they stood there and looked.

Now a branch full of *cucurito* came crashing down.

"Ahhhhhhh!" they shouted. "Here comes our food."

When the branch fell, it killed someone. It fell on the head of a boy, Wade's son.

Now a branch full of *pijiguao* fell.

"Ahhhh!" they shouted. "Our food!"

When it fell, it landed right on the nose of Odoma, the paca. He ran off screaming and yelling. He had his face crushed. The pacas are still that way today, with flat faces. That's the reason why. You can see them.

Then another branch fell, and another and another. They were falling all over. The people got crushed, killed.

They just ran, terrified. They didn't know where to go. The whole Earth was covered. Wherever they went, fruit was falling, crushing them.

That's what they say.

SEMENIA

Wanadi was still living here on Earth, in Wade's house. They gathered around him, weeping, asking for help.

Wanadi said: "Okay. Now I'll make new people. I'll make birds to help you. They'll have wings to fly up to the branches. They'll get the fruit."

At that time there were no birds. That was in the beginning.

Wanadi stuck a few rows of sticks in the earth and looked at them. He sat down in front of them, smoking. He played his maraca. He sang. He thought.

That's the way he made his new people for the harvest, his new people called birds. When they wanted to, they turned into birds and flew. Then they changed back into people like us again.

Now the birds made ladders out of vines. Some went climbing up them like people. They climbed up the vines. Others flew up to the branches like birds. Now they started gathering the fruit. The old people watched them from the ground. They wove *tudi*. The birds began to come. They were carrying the fruit. It was heavy. It started to slip and fall. It killed people like before.

"That's no good," said one of the birds. "We'll plant. We'll cultivate the earth. We can help. We're strong, us birds. Let's stop this gathering and cut down the tree. Then we'll plant in the earth."

That was the chief of the birds. His name is Semenia. He was wise. He showed us how to plant. They cut the trees down. That's how they make *conucos*. That's how they plant. The old people didn't know that. They only knew how to gather wild fruit, like monkeys. When Semenia came, he showed them how to cut down trees to make *conucos*. When they cut down the Marahuaka tree, they fed the earth. Semenia showed them how to work to get their food.

132

There were two who didn't want to obey. They didn't want to work. They were called Mado, the jaguar, and Wachedi, the tapir.

"Who's that giving orders now?" they asked. "Everyone's obeying. Well, we don't want to work or obey. When we're hungry, we just find our food and eat it, that's all. We're not going to have anything to do with those people."

They went looking for fallen fruit. They ate. They gorged themselves. What was left they were going to hide. They thought: "We two are the biggest ones on Earth. The others are so small. Semenia is tiny. How can we obey him? How can we share?"

They hid the food in caves. They went back to get more. They weren't thinking of the others. They were their own chiefs. They worked alone. They didn't want to share because they were so hungry. They didn't listen to Semenia when he said: "First we work together; then we celebrate. We'll divide the food later."

In the old days Semenia was our chief. They said: "Why's he chief?"

The people watched them. Semenia watched them. "That's no good," he said. "Those two are hiding food. They don't want to live with us. They've forgotten we're here. They're making fun of us. Now we'll punish them."

Then he called for them. At first they didn't want to come. Then everyone circled around them, staring at them. They were afraid. Then they went to see Semenia.

"You're working?" he asked.

"Oh, yeh. We're working," they answered.

"Good. That's why I called. We all work together. Now we're thirsty. There's no water here. You're going to go to the Casiquiare to get water for us."

"Okay," they said. They were scared now. The others were watching them.

Semenia gave them a strainer to carry the water in. It was a trick. You can't carry water in a strainer. They were both idiots. They didn't catch on.

"Okay," they said. They went walking and walking, far off there on the Casiquiare trail to get water with a strainer.

Semenia wanted hunger and misery to stop. That's why he came with his new people, with the birds. Wanadi made them. The people were living in hunger and misery because of Odosha. They were listening to Odosha. They weren't together. There was no order, no justice.

They were all selfish. They had no chiefs. Each one just found his own dirt and ate it. They didn't worry about anyone else. They never thought about the others.

Semenia made himself chief to teach us. He showed us how to work. He punished the ones that didn't want to live like people, like brothers. He brought food, rain, fertility and obedience for everyone. He showed them what to do. Now we have food again. We're happy despite Odosha. Semenia was Wanadi's messenger, our first chief in the beginning.

When Jaguar and Tapir left, Semenia said: "Now we'll cut it down."

Four toucans came up. They were like people in the beginning. They brought some good axes to cut down Marahuaka. They hit the trunk. Their axes bounced off. The tree was thick. The wood was hard. The tree wouldn't go down. The axes couldn't cut it. Now they turned into birds, toucans with long, hard beaks. They were their axes now. They tried to peck the tree down. Nothing. They couldn't do it. The first toucan broke the edge of his beak. That's the way the toucans are now, with beaks like saws. Then another toucan came up, and another and another. Nothing. Then the woodpeckers came. Wanadi came up to peck like Wanadi tonoro. Semenia came as a Semenia bird. Waraihai and Sumunuadi came too. They went at the tree with their beaks. They cut all day. At night, they rested. They slept. When the sun rose, they got up. The tree was intact again as if nothing had happened.

"What are we going to do?" they asked. "We can't go to sleep. Our cuts just close up. We're just wasting our time. We'll never finish."

Semenia said: "We won't cut this way anymore, all at the same time. We'll take turns now. One will cut and the others will rest."

So that's what they did. There was always one cutting, day and night. The cut didn't close. They kept on cutting deeper and deeper, first one, then the other. They just kept on cutting. They slept too, first one, then the other. They didn't get tired. Peck . . . peck . . . peck . . . peck. They pecked like that for days.

Now one of them came up. He gave the last blow. It was Wanadi. He was happy. "It's done!" he shouted.

It really was done. It was completely cut.

They all turned to look. They were frightened. "It's going to fall now. Which way is it going to fall? Which way should we run?"

Marahuaka didn't fall. It just stood there, hanging from the Sky in silence. It was just there. It wouldn't budge.

They all stood there looking.

"What was all that work for?" That tree just wouldn't fall. They couldn't understand it.

Now they called Kadiio, the squirrel. "Run up there and see what's happening."

"Okay," said Kadiio. And he went running up to see. Then he came back down. "It's tangled up there in the Sky," he said. "The branches are caught. They look like roots up there. That's why it's hanging. It's stuck."

Semenia gave him an axe. "Go up and cut it."

Kadiio cut Marahuaka. He cut it up there in Heaven. It was an upside down tree, with its roots on top.

Then the great Marahuaka tree finally fell. The entire Earth shook. Branches, fruit, palms, seeds, everything fell. It felt like the sky was falling. It was like the end of the world.

They hid in caves. They huddled together. They shut their eyes. They were afraid.

Then they came out. When they came out it was raining everywhere. They didn't know what it was. It was the first rain. It fell from Heaven in waterfalls and rapids. It poured down from Heaven out of Marahuaka's cut roots.

"Rain," said Semenia. "Now we can plant."

The water looked for a way through the Earth. Now new paths, the rivers, were born. The Orinoco, Fhadamu, Kunukunuma, Antawari, Merewari, Metakuni, Kuntinama, and others, many others. All the rivers were born. They called them the New Water. They ran like snakes across the Earth.

The earth became very soft for planting. Now the women gathered cuttings, shoots, sprouts, seeds. They gathered them in the rain to plant.

Now four waterfalls came down from the top of Marahuaka, from the cliffs: Motasha, Iamo, Namanama, and Kuhuaka. They were born on the green Earth and they opened beautiful ways.

In Kushamakari, three waterfalls were searching for paths, Auakosho, Iukati, and Matuhushi. They ran along pulling up stones and shooting out foam. You couldn't recognize the Earth anymore from the beginning.

Now there were buds everywhere. The Earth became green. The forest bloomed, our *conucos* blossomed. The forest filled with trees. Our *conucos* filled with yuca.

Marahuaka's trunk broke into three pieces. We call them Marahu-aka huha, Marahuaka huih and Atawashiho. They turned into stone when they fell. Now they're mountains, the three parts of the highest mountain on Earth. They're there as reminders. It was that day that our food came.

Kadiio fell down too, onto one of the Duida's peaks. Now he lives there, hidden. He's the master of that peak they call Kadiio ewiti.

The people were happy; happy together in their *conuco*. The yuca grew quickly. All of a sudden it was there. Now the men rested. That's what Semenia told them. Now the women worked. That's how we still do it. We don't forget that way. The men clear the *conuco*, like Marahuaka in the beginning. The women plant and harvest and prepare it.

Now they came carrying *wuwa* filled with yuca. Then the men worked again. They wove baskets, strainers, trays, presses. They carved graters and *kanawa*. Those are their jobs. The women harvest, carry, grate, press, cook the cassava. They make *iarake* in the *kanawa*.

"That's good," said Semenia. Then he said: "Let's dance. Let's sing and eat and drink. Now we'll remember."

It was the first harvest festival. The Conuco Song, that's what they call it, *Adahe ademi hidi*, that's its name.

Now they played the *momi* bark horns and Semenia sang. Wanadi and Wade sang too. They remembered everything. They didn't forget anything: Kuchi, Dodoima, Kamaso, Marahuaka, how they planted, how they cleared. *Watunna*, that's what we call the memory of our beginning.

Just as they sang, we sing now.

The *aichudiaha*, the old ones of today, they know the ancient ways. They sing and teach the young ones what Semenia did. They teach us how to work so that our food returns. They sing about how Jaguar and Tapir were punished.

It's always the same, now as before. The way we ate once, we do over and over again. We obey. We remember. The old ones sing beautifully. We just repeat.

Now those people who came to help in the beginning, those people that Wanadi made to cut down Marahuaka, said goodby.

As they were dancing and singing, they turned into birds of every color. They flew off. The air was filled with feathers, all red and green and yellow and blue. It was beautiful. Now the Water Mother, Huiio, the Great Snake, came leaping out of the water and shot into the air.

"I want my crown," she said, looking for birds and feathers for her crown. Huiio threw her great body into the sky. Many birds came. She covered herself with feathers. She was the rainbow. They called it *wasudi*.

"Good. It's done," the birds said. "Let's leave now."

Then they disappeared. They went to Heaven. They just left their bodies on the Earth for the birds of today. You couldn't see the rainbow anymore. It went to live in Lake Akuena.

Semenia went off as a bird too. He looked like the Wanadi bird. He was kin to Wanadi. Now he's the master of the Earth's food.

Okay. That's it.

MADO
and WACHEDI

They were watching out there, jealous. They were mad. They were hungry. They saw the people happily eating. They were out in the forest, far away, up in a tree, just watching from far away.

Those people didn't want anything to do with them.

"They tricked us," said Mado. "We were wasting our time getting water with that strainer. We tried bringing it, but nothing. The water just went right through that strainer. We just kept trying and the water kept falling through. They made us go to fool us. Marahuaka fell when we were gone out there. Semenia didn't want us to get any food. He doesn't want to share with us."

"That's right," Wachedi answered. He was sad. He saw the feast and the rainbow.

When Marahuaka fell, those two were at the Old Water. They were afraid to come back without any water.

When it fell, when it rained, they said: "What's that? They cut it down. They tricked us. Come on, let's go. We'll be left with nothing."

They couldn't get there. The path was different now; full of trees, trees and roots and thickets and thorns. They were hardly going anywhere. When they had come, there wasn't anything on the path. Now it was jungle all over. They were lost. They didn't know the way now. All they could see were trees. Then they came to a river and then another and another. "How'll we get across?" they said. They got across swimming, one right after the other. Then they heard the music, the bark horns, the laughter, the singing. They climbed up a tree and looked.

"Okay," said Mado. "*So'to aihede, huasa!* Now we're going to eat people, brother-in-law!"

He turned into a jaguar. He went off and started eating people in revenge. That was in the beginning. Now jaguars are evil. They eat people. They say that's the way it began.

Wachedi didn't hear very well. He heard: "*Suhua dumina konoko aihede, huasa.* Now we're going to eat leaves and roots, brother-in-law."

"Good," he said.

He turned into a tapir. He went off and started eating leaves and roots. That's what tapirs eat today. That was in the beginning. It's lucky for us he didn't hear very well.

Now Wachedi climbed up Marahuaka, up to the highest part of the mountain. We call it Marahuaka huih. That's where he stayed to live. He's the grandfather, the master of the tapirs of today. Now we go there to hunt them. There are lots of big ones. They serve as food for people. That's their punishment.

That's all now.

WAHNATU

WAHNATU

They sang and danced and drank for five full days and nights. They were drunk, those birds, those old people. Now their *Wanwanna*, their Falling Tree Festival, came to an end and they began to leave. Semenia spread out his wings and flew off. The other birds followed him. They left their forms and colors here for the birds of the Earth today. Those are their signs. They went to live like people up in the Sky. That's why they call them Kahuhana, Sky People. Kamaso left his form here for the Kamaso bird. That's what we call it. Huiio, the Great Snake, flew off too. She left *wasudi*, the rainbow, here as her sign. You can see it in the rain and sunlight. Those Kahuhana went to Lake Akuena, the Sea of Heaven. It circles the entire Earth from East to West and West to East. The water that poured down from the Marahuaka tree came from there. When the old people left, they left the shoots and buds of food at the foot of Marahuaka, in Wade's black soil. They just left it there growing wild. Wade went away too. He just left his form down here. Now the sloths have it. The masters of all the other animals went too. The only ones left here were the animals of today.

Now Wanadi thought: "Okay. How will I keep that food from getting lost? It's just been left there. Those animals are only signs. They don't know how to take care of food. I'll have to make another person to stay here on Earth and take care of it."

He went to Mount Dekuhana and found some clay. He beat it. He shaped it. He dried it with fire and made it hard. Then he took his maraca and lit his cigar. He sang. He blew. And that's how he made Wahnatu, the first man, the grandfather of the *so'to*. Like a clay doll, he made him.

"You're a *so'to*," he told him. "You'll make *conucos* so you don't go hungry. You'll watch after what the old people planted."

Now, with the same clay, he made Wetashi, the first woman. He made her for Wahnatu, to plant in Wahnatu's *conuco*. Then he made a house for them.

That's what happened. The *so'to* went to Wade's at the foot of Mount Marahuaka. He cleared the trees and brush. He got the *conuco* ready for Wetashi to plant. Then he went back home. "I cut down all the trees. The *conuco*'s ready. Now we'll have the festival. Make the *iarake*. I'm going. I'll be back soon."

Wahnatu went up into the mountains to find bark to make a *siwo* horn with. He made it just like Semenia did when he called all the birds and animals to begin the Falling Tree Festival after they cut down the Marahuaka tree. Now Wahnatu blew on the *siwo*: "Woooo-woooo-woooo." It was the same Semenia voice hidden in the *siwo*.

Now all those Kahuhana, the masters of all the birds and animals, came down from the Sky Place. They were the ones who cut down the first tree. They came down singing and dancing. "What are you, Semenia here on Earth?" they asked Wahnatu. "Did you call? Here we are. You cleared the people's *conuco*? We'll celebrate with you. Now you'll be the *ademi* (song) master, the *wanwanna* (dance) master. We'll show you how to make the *wasaha* (dance stick)."

The *wasaha* keeps the rhythm. You beat it on the Earth and it calls the food spirits that live down there.

Now they went into the forest to find the *wasaha* tree. They cut it and hung two deer hooves from it. It sounded like a maraca. They got *wanna* and made the *tekoye* horns with it. Then they made drums and dance maracas. And they showed him how to cut *rako rako* which are the little bamboo flutes. Now they began blowing and playing and singing. "That's our voice," they said. "This is so you can learn our words, the exact song, the story of what we did when we cut down Marahuaka. Listen. Then repeat it. Don't forget. Later, call us when you go back to your house and we'll come and dance. We'll protect the seeds your woman plants in the *conuco*."

Then each bird *sadashe* (master) gave Wahnatu some feathers from his own family. He had beautiful reds and blues and yellows. The animal masters told him: "We'll dress ourselves in them to dance." They took the feathers and stuck them in their ear lobes. Wahnatu watched them and did the same thing. Then they found wild cotton to make cords with. They tied huge curassow and macaw feathers to them and made *womo ansai*. They hung the *womo ansai* down their backs.

Wahnatu just watched everything they did. Then he made his own *ansai* and hung it down his back. Now the animal *sadashe* got *wasai* palms and cut them in long strips and tied them together. That's how they made the *wasai iaddi*, the dance skirts. They made the *wemue*, the dance hats, with *wasai* too. They tied on big, beautiful feathers and put them on their heads. Wahnatu watched them and did the same thing. Now they got their *chakara* and took out beautiful little seed maraca and blue and white glass beads which they had bought at Wanadi's store on the shore of Dama. They made long pendants with them and attached feathers and hung them from their arms. "These are called *ahötte*," they told Wahnatu. And they gave him seeds and beads to make his own *ahötte*. Then they found *wishu* and *tununu* trees and cut off the barks and squeezed out the juices and painted their bodies all over with them. They made drawings for the food masters. Wahnatu copied them.

Now the peccary master told Wahnatu: "I'm the Mountain Spirit, the *so'to*'s house spirit. Here's my sign. This is my power." And he gave him a beautiful collar made out of peccary teeth. Wahnatu took it and put it around his neck.

The Kahuhana said goodby to Wahnatu: "We're going. We'll come back later. Go home now. When the *iarake*'s ready, call us with your *siwo* horn. That horn is the voice of Semenia, our master. We'll come right away. Then we'll dance with you."

And that's how Wahnatu received the *Watunna*, the wisdom of the old people, when he met them that first time up in the mountains. He was happy as he went home. He raced along the path, his dance stick banging along the ground with the deer hooves saying "shhhi . . . shhhi" and his seeds and maracas "boook . . . boook" and his collars answering "kreek . . . kreek" and his dance skirt "srop . . . srop."

When he was nearly home, he blew the *siwo*: "Woooo . . . woooo . . . woooo." Wetashi, his wife, came out to meet him with a gourd full of *iarake*.

"You're beautiful," she said to him as she looked at all his drawings and feathers, his collars, his skirt, his hat. She didn't recognize him. "Are you Semenia?" she asked. Then they put gourds filled with *iarake* all over the ground and Wahnatu called the old people with his *siwo*. "Your *iarake* is here waiting for you," is what the *siwo* was saying. But the woman, Wetashi, she didn't understand it. She just heard: "Woooo . . . woooo . . . woooo."

The bird and animal masters started arriving. Wahnatu saw them. He drank and celebrated with them. But Wetashi didn't see them. First they sang the *Adahe ademi hidi,* the *Watunna* that tells the story of Marahuaka and how they cut it down. Wahnatu listened. Wetashi couldn't hear anything. Wahnatu repeated it. Now the woman heard. But she thought it was Semenia that was singing. She thought Wahnatu was dancing all alone. She couldn't see all the other dancers that had come down from Heaven to dance with him.

That was the first *Wanwanna* Festival for us *so'to.*

KAHIURU

After our first grandfather, Wahnatu, Wanadi went to make other people, other houses. He walked all over. He looked around for a good place. Then he came to Maipures Rapids on the Orinoco. It was a good place. Wanadi made the Fañuru (Spanish) people right on the shore there. He wanted to make their house. He didn't have time. His enemy, Odosha, came up there.

From the beginning of things, Odosha had been chasing Wanadi. He wanted to kill him. He wanted to destroy everything he did. Wanadi was moving fast. Odosha just kept on looking and looking. He couldn't find him. He would always come too late. He just found his tracks there, that's all. Wanadi had already gone.

Finally he found Wanadi at Maipures, as he was about to make the Fañuru's house. Odosha let out a big laugh. He thought: "I've finally caught him." Wanadi saw him. He thought: "Odosha's here. I'm going. I'll come back later and make the Fañuru's house." Then he went down river to the mouth of the Atabapo. He made the Winavi (Puinave Indians) there. Then he made their house, a big, beautiful one. It was called Marakuhaña.

Odosha tricked the Fañuru in the beginning. He spoke to the white men. They were sad, abandoned. They didn't have any houses. Odosha told them: "Wanadi is evil. He made you poor. He left you with nothing. Then he went and made a beautiful village for some other people further down. That's not right. You should make war on them and take their houses. What Wanadi did isn't right. You should kill him."

As soon as they heard that, right away they marched against Marakuhaña. They beat the people with clubs. They killed them. They stayed in the village. Then they went looking for Wanadi, to kill him.

Wanadi had left down the Orinoco. That's how war, injustice, and theft began. That's how evil came. The Fañuru heard Odosha. They stopped being Wanadi's people.

Kahiuru was their first chief. He was the first soldier. Odosha set him against Wanadi.

Wanadi came to Ankosturaña (Angostura). He made very large, good houses there. It was a rich, beautiful village. Then Wanadi made another white man, like Fañuru. He was called Iaranavi. He filled Ankosturaña with those people. That's why those people are called Ankosturañankomo, Angostura people.

Wanadi made Iaranavi very wise like Fañuru. But Odosha ruined the other one. He was no good now. That's why Wanadi made another one, a new one. He gave him riches, goods of every kind: iron, cloth, shirts, guns, machetes, everything. He gave him money too. He told him: "You're a merchant." That's what he told Iaranavi.

He was the rich man, Wanadi's shopkeeper, friend to the poor. He was always travelling around, trading goods. Our grandfathers travelled to Ankosturaña too to get goods from Iaranavi. They learned how to trade there, how to exchange their stuff for the things they didn't have.

Wanadi said: "Good. It's done. Now I'm going far away." He walked way off to the East. It was far. He came to the Amenadi (Essequibo). Then he went down river till he came to the shore of Dama, the sea. He sat down when he got there. He started thinking, dreaming. Now he thought: "Okay. The Earth ends here. Good, another village, very good, another white man, very good."

He dreamt. He made that village called Amenadiña. He dreamt another white man: "Rich, rich, strong, very wise." He was called Hurunko, the Dutch man. That's how he did it.

Now he went off to the West, walking and walking. He came to a mountain called Karaka hidi. He made a big, beautiful village there with lots of houses. They call it Karakaña (Caracas).

Kahiuru, the chief of the Fañuru, heard about it. He thought: "Let's go find Wanadi. Let's rob that village, Karakaña." He gathered up his people, his soldiers. They walked and walked. That's how they came there.

"We're here," they said. "Whose village is this?"

"Mine," answered Wanadi.

"This isn't yours," they said. "It's ours. Everything on Earth is ours." That's what the Spaniards told Wanadi when they arrived in Karakaña with Kahiuru. They only had clubs to fight with. They didn't have bows or arrows or anything. They were very poor, naked. They didn't have anything. They just had hate and envy because of what Odosha had told them. They wanted to rob Karakaña like they had robbed Marakuhaña. They wanted to kill Wanadi.

"I'm Wanadi," he answered. "I made you. I made everything. You don't belong to Odosha. He's a liar. He tricked you. It's no good what you've done. Don't fight against me. Don't rob the other people. Now I'll give you yours, your houses and everything else."

"Get out of here," said Kahiuru. "We don't want anything to do with you. We're not your people. The Earth isn't yours. It's ours."

He said what Odosha had told him to say.

They grabbed Wanadi. Kahiuru tied him up to a post with *mamure* cane. The soldiers were all around him. Now they took him up to the mountain outside the village. They left him there to die. Then they went back to Karakaña to rob the houses. They were empty. The Fañuru settled there. They left Wamedi, the rooster, to watch Wanadi. When Wanadi died, he was supposed to call them. "HE'S DEAD!" That's what they told him to shout.

Wanadi couldn't die. They didn't know that. He was wise, powerful. One day went by, then another and another. He didn't eat. He didn't drink. He didn't die. The guard watched. Nothing. He waited. Nothing.

Now Wanadi dreamed: "Free, free, I'm free." He got loose through the power of his dream. He left the cane hanging there on the post. He just went. He went back to his father-in-law's house in Kushamakari.

The guard he turned into a rooster. He was the first Wamedi. When he screamed, he screamed like a rooster.

"Wanadi nistama!" he screamed. "Wanadi's gone!" That's the way roosters still sing. They sing that way as a reminder.

Now the soldiers got there and they asked: "How did he get away?" They couldn't figure it out.

"Here I am," he said when he got back to Kushamakari.

"What happened?" they asked him. "Where were you?"

"Over there," he said. "Just making houses, making people."

He didn't tell them anything else. They gave him something to eat. They were very happy when he got back from Karakaña.

Now the sun came up and Wanadi said "I'm going." He went out hunting and fishing. He brought home food. They ate. They were happy. He slept in the house with Kaweshawa, his wife, again.

When the sun rose, he told her: "I'm going over there."

Now he went up the Orinoco by canoe to make new people and houses. He wanted more and more people to fight Odosha and Kahiuru, the Odoshankomo and the Fañuru.

When he said "I'm going," Odosha was listening. He was listening from his house. He thought: "Okay. Kahiuru couldn't kill him in Karakaña. That's why he's back. Now I'll kill him." He followed him up the Orinoco.

Wanadi paddled up river. He was dreaming lots of people, smoking tobacco, singing, playing maraca. Odosha just stayed behind him, watching everything he did. Now Wanadi got some red dirt. He blew tobacco smoke. He made those *wiriki* in his maraca sing. He made Shirishana (Guaika-Yanoamo). Those people were good in the beginning when Wanadi blew them to life. He built them a huge house on the banks of the Orinoco. "It's done," he said. Then he went up river.

Now Odosha came up to Shirishana's house with Wanadi's face on in order to fool him. "Here I am," he said. "I'm Wanadi. Now you're going to be strong and wise. Over there on Wanaio hidi (Mount Guanayo) lives a *huhai*. His name is Mamaku. He's very powerful. If you eat him, you'll be wise and powerful."

And that's what he did, the first one, the grandfather of the Shirishana. Odosha tricked him. He went with his people to find Mamaku. He killed him. He ate him. Mamaku wasn't a good *huhai*. He was a sorcerer, an evil witch-doctor. When he ate him, Shirishana went crazy. He kept his human form but that's all. His spirit turned into an animal. He moved around like an animal. He thought like an animal. He lost his mind. He hid in the mountains, naked. He didn't know how to do anything anymore, just kill and rob real people. And that's the way his grandchildren stayed. They go around without loincloths. They don't make houses. They don't make anything. They don't have hammocks, strainers, baskets, blowguns, canoes, or anything. That's why they come and rob us; because they don't have anything to give us for our things. They don't cultivate. They just eat meat and wild fruit. They don't know how to do anything except scream and jump and yell like howler monkeys. They take everything they see. They beat men and they steal women.

They started when they ate Mamaku. They came to rob and kill our grandfathers. The old ones chased them into the mountains to punish them and get back their women. They looked for their houses, their villages. They didn't have any. They ran around the jungle like peccary. At night they slept in the trees. They just covered themselves with *bijao* leaves and slept in the vines.

One night they surprised them with the women they had stolen. They shot arrows at them. They woke up. They hid behind the women. They pushed them in front of them. The old ones stopped shooting in order not to kill the women. The Shirishana escaped and gathered together again. Our grandfathers set a termite nest on fire and threw it at them. The whole forest was filled with smoke. The Shirishana were weeping and coughing. They let the women go.

Wanadi thought: "Okay. Shirishana is lost. Odosha's behind me. There's nothing I can do now." He went back to Kushamakari.

When he arrived, he found Kahiuru and his people. They had come from Karakaña to find him. They grabbed him. They tied him up. They took him prisoner back to Karakaña.

There was nothing there but soldiers; soldiers and police. They had something to kill with, called gunpowder. They had mountains of it. They wanted to kill Wanadi with it but he blew on the gunpowder and turned it into a cloud. They were blinded. There was no more gunpowder then. "What'll we do now?" they thought. "That man is strong. How will we kill him?" Many tried. First one came to kill him, then another and another and still another. They couldn't. Then lots of soldiers came up and made a circle around him. When they did that, Wanadi began dreaming strange animals. First pigs. There were soldiers hidden in all the houses in Karakaña. Wanadi went to one house. He opened the door. He called. Some soldiers came out. Wanadi dreamed: "Cows, cattle." He turned them into cattle. He went to another house. It was filled with soldiers. He opened the door. He dreamed: "Horses." And horses came out instead of soldiers. And so he went to all the houses one after the other. There were hardly any soldiers or people left. There were just herds of pigs and cattle and horses. Later on, the Fañuru had many more animals, descended from those first ones. Wanadi made them, when those people wanted to kill him in Karakaña.

Some soldiers escaped and hid. There weren't many. Kahiuru jumped out with them and caught Wanadi by surprise. Now some other men who were hidden called Fadre (*padres*, priests) came out too.

"Who are you?" they asked him. "Where do you come from? Who's your father?"

"I'm Wanadi," he answered. "I come from Kahuña (Heaven). My father is Wanadi."

The Fadre didn't like that answer. "You're a liar! You're not Wanadi. You're Odosha," they said.

"I'm Wanadi," he said again. "*Wanadi inedi*, Wanadi's son. I'm Wanadi's *damodede*. He sent me here as chief."

"You're lying," they said to him. "And for that lie we're going to kill you."

Then they began whipping him with vines, asking: "Whose village is this? Whose house? Whose Earth is this?"

"It's all mine," said Wanadi. "I made it all. I made you too."

"Liar! It's all ours. Nothing is yours. We're going to punish you for that."

And they beat him again.

Then Kahiuru said: "Okay. We couldn't kill him with gunpowder. Now we'll try again."

He sent for a post to hang him from. It was shaped like a forked *Kruza ake* (cross). That's what they called it. When they brought *Kruza ake*, they nailed him there with iron points. "That way he won't escape," they thought.

"It's done," they said. "Now let's leave him on the road to die."

"Good," said Kahiuru. "Now he's going to die." Kahiuru was strong too. He knew a lot. He didn't like Wanadi. He called Wamedi, the rooster. He sent him to the mountain to watch *Kruza ake* and tell them when Wanadi died. "'Wanadi's dead' is what you'll sing," he told him.

They stayed in Karakaña, waiting for Wamedi's call.

When the sun rose, Wamedi sang. "Wanadi nistama!" he screamed. "Wanadi's gone!" That's what he sang. He didn't sing the death song. He sang "He's gone," and that's all.

Kahiuru, the Fadre, and the soldiers came to see what happened. They looked at *Kruza ake*. Wanadi was hanging there. He wasn't moving. He was dead. He was there.

"Here he is," they said.

Rooster went right on singing. He was singing: "Wanadi's gone!"

"He isn't gone," they said, yelling at Wamedi. "He's right here."

"Wanadi's gone!" Three times Wamedi sang that way.

"Shut up!" said Kahiuru. "You're a liar. You're a worthless guard."

Wanadi was like a corpse. It was a trick. He had already gone. He had taken his *damodede* out of the body. He had gone back to Kushamakari. Wamedi knew that. The Fadre and the Fañuru didn't. Wanadi was just hanging there like an empty shell. It was just his body. He had gone back to Kushamakari. Wamedi didn't sing anymore. They beat him with sticks and clubs.

When Wanadi arrived, Kaweshawa and his in-laws rejoiced. They called all the people together. "Wanadi isn't dead!" they shouted. People came from all over to celebrate.

In Karakaña, the Fañuru stopped looking. "We killed him," the Fadre said. "It wasn't Wanadi. It was Odosha. We punished him. We beat him."

They kept *Kruza ake* as proof, as a sign. That's their reminder. Later, they made lots of crosses. They like to make crosses to show people. They say: "On this post he died." They didn't know. They don't know. They say they killed him. It's not true. They couldn't. He tricked them and got away.

ANKOSTURAÑA

Ankosturaña was a big, beautiful village. The Iaranavi lived there. They were Wanadi's people, good people, rich and happy.

One day an Ankosturañankomo, one of those people from there, dreamed about Odosha. Evil got hold of him. When he woke up, he wanted to fight. He was mad. He shouted terrible words from the dream. He cursed his daughter. He spoke very badly to her. That was the sign that Iaranavi was lost. It was the first madness and it brought ruin.

"Slut! Tramp!" that man screamed at his daughter. "I hope Kahiuru comes from Karakaña. I hope he takes you away to live with him."

In Karakaña, Kahiuru heard that Iaranavi's dreaming madness. He came to Ankosturaña. He took the girl away.

Karakaña had hardly any people, just lots of pigs and horses and cows. There were a few soldiers, a few Fadre. There were no women. Almost all the houses were empty. Kahiuru was sad.

As soon as he brought the woman back, Kahiuru began sleeping with her over and over again. The Iaranavi girl had lots of children. That was the beginning of the Karakañankomo, the Caracas people. That's the way Karakaña was filled up with new people.

The good people, the Iaranavi, began to mix with the bad people, the Fañuru, in Karakaña. Half-breeds were born. They were like Fañuru, like their father, Kahiuru, people of Odosha, not Wanadi. A few came out good, like their mother.

Kahiuru said: "Good. Now we're strong, like in the beginning. We're all soldiers. We're poor. We don't have anything. Iaranavi is rich. He has money, iron, cloth. He has everything. He's Wanadi's man. Wanadi gave him everything. We don't have anything. Let's go to

Ankosturaña. Let's fight them. The Earth is ours, not theirs. We'll fix them."

They came to the shore of the Uriñaku (Orinoco) in front of Ankosturaña. The river was very wide. Ankosturaña was on the other side. They couldn't get across. They just stood there shouting and screaming on the north shore of the river. They didn't have canoes. They just got in the water and started swimming. All they had to fight with were clubs.

When the Ankosturañankomo saw them in the river, they thought: "They've come to fight. Let's fight." They shot at them with *arakusa* (arquebusses). They had lots of *arakusa*. They killed lots of them. As they killed them, the bodies fell in the river; first one, then another and another and another, lots of them. They lined up like a bridge. Now, from the north shore, the Fañuru all began walking across the bridge. They all crossed. That's how they got to the other side, to Ankosturaña, by walking over the bodies. As they crossed, the bodies turned into stone. You can still see them in the Orinoco in front of Ankosturaña. They call them the "Center Stone."

Many Fañuru died as they came across. They killed them with *arakusa*. They had nothing but clubs. But they were many, that's why they won. They killed the men. They raped the women. They mixed the races again. That's how the Iaranavi were destroyed. It put an end to the good people in Ankosturaña.

The Karakañankomo got money, houses, iron, everything. "Now we're rich," they said.

Trading was finished. The Fañuru didn't have any traders. They only had soldiers.

Now new people were born. There were lots and lots of new babies. Because of their fathers, they came out bad, thieves and liars.

Some of the Iaranavi hid in the jungle and were saved. Some women escaped too. They didn't want to sleep with the Fañuru. There are still many good people near Ankosturaña, in the outskirts, the villages. They're descendants of Iaranavi, poor people, good like us, our friends.

Now when people from over there come looking for us, they say to us: "Let's cut wood and gather rubber." Some of them aren't liars. They pay well and they're good. We say: "That's Iaranavi." Others fool us. They make us work. Then they don't pay. They don't treat us right. We say: "Here's Fañuru."

With the Fañuru came a people called Kurumankomo, the black people. They were servants of the others. Their father was a black man named Mekuru. He was Kahiuru's servant. They were good, poor people too. The Fañuru made them work. They didn't give them any money. Lots of them ran off to the jungle and mixed with Iaranavi. That's how the Murunmatto, the mestizos, were born. They have our color. They're our friends.

MAHAIWADI

When they took Ankosturaña, the Fañuru said: "Okay. Now we're the masters. We're the rich ones. We have the *arakusa* and the machetes. Now we're going to take more land, more villages. We're going to kill Wanadi's people."

They went into the jungle, up the Orinoco and the Caura. They came to our lands, robbing houses, killing people, eating them. They ate human flesh. They just came to rob and kill.

Some of them went to Marakuhaña (San Fernando de Atabapo). That's where their fathers had come from. Others went to Meraraña (La Esmeralda). They left soldiers there with cannons and gunpowder. They went up the Ventuari and the Kunukunuma, up our rivers. They made the men and women prisoners. They forced the men to work. They didn't pay them. They raped the women. The old ones couldn't live anymore because of them.

Many were taken prisoner in Marakuhaña, in Meraraña. They worked. They didn't eat. Many of them died.

A Fadre came to Meraraña. He brought *Kruza ake* there. He showed it to our grandfathers. He said: "Wanadi's dead. He died on this post. He wasn't Wanadi. He was Odosha. He was a fake. That's why we killed him. Now we're the masters of the Earth. There's no more Iaranavi. The money, the *arakusa*, the iron, the cloth, they're all ours."

He just said that to trick our grandfathers, so they would think Wanadi was dead. They knew. They weren't fooled.

The Fañuru came in canoes. They went up the Merevari, the Antawari, the Fhadamu, the Davarehudi. They were looking for people to kill and eat.

Mahaiwadi said: "Okay. Those men are very evil. We're going to throw them out."

157

"How can we?" they asked. "They're strong. They know too much. We don't have *arakusa,* iron. We only have bows and arrows."

Mahaiwadi lived on the banks of the Arahame. He was very wise. He was a *huhai.* He took his *damodede* out of his body. No one saw him. He hid in the jungle, playing maraca, singing, smoking. He went to the mouths of the Arahame, the Kuntinama, and the Tamatama. He threw tobacco leaves and *wiriki* all around there. He called the *mawadi.* Then he went to the Kashishare (Casiquiare). He threw his maraca in and hid in the forest. He just stayed there singing and smoking.

The Fañuru's canoes turned over and the *mawadi* ate them. Some of them left their canoes and ran into the jungle. Mahaiwadi lay down in his hammock. He left his body there as a trick. He went out in a new body, like a jaguar. He sent the jaguar into the forest to eat the Fañuru. Mahaiwadi was sleeping, dreaming. His jaguar ran after the Fañuru. It ate one, then another and another and another. Mahaiwadi just lay there in his hammock as if he were dead.

The Fañuru had lots of gold. Before they died they buried it at the foot of Mount Wana hidi where the Kuntinama and the Huidoni meet. When they buried the gold, they turned into carved stones. You can still see them in Wana hidi, but you can't touch them. They're filled with poison.

Mahaiwadi's jaguar ran to tell the people. He screamed: "The Fañuru are in my stomach. You can come out of your caves now."

Mahaiwadi woke up. He turned into a bird and took off singing: "Free, free, I'm free." That's how he sang.

When Mahaiwadi died, a star crossed the sky. They say his *damodede* was returning to Heaven. They keep Mahaiwadi's skull and bones in the Arahame as proof, as a reminder. They have power. They cure the sick.

AMENADIÑA

Wanadi went to the edge of the Earth, to the shore of the sea, to find Hurunko and his village, Amenadiña.

Hurunko was wise and powerful. He was a good man. Odosha hadn't come to his village. Neither had Kahiuru.

Wanadi sat down to think. He thought: "This man's been saved." Then he thought about Ankosturaña, about Iaranavi: "That one's been lost. I'll make a test to save him."

Now he called Iaranavi dreaming. Far away in Ankosturaña, Iaranavi dreamed too. He heard him. When the sun rose, he said: "I'm going. Wanadi's at the edge of the sea. He's calling me. That's how I dreamed."

He went off walking and walking. He walked all the way to Amenadiña.

"You're here," said Wanadi. "I called you to go to Heaven to visit my mother. She lives in Heaven. I want to know how she is."

He gave Iaranavi a horse and money to buy the horse food along the way.

"Okay," Iaranavi said. He got on his horse. He didn't go to Heaven to find Kumariawa. He went and hid. He didn't spend the money. He just sat there waiting and didn't do anything. Then he came back and said: "I saw your mother, Kumariawa."

"How is she?" Wanadi asked.

"Fine," Iaranavi said. "She's happy."

"Does she have food?" asked Wanadi.

"Oh, yes. Lots of food."

"What does she eat?"

"She eats mangoes," answered Iaranavi.

Wanadi became furious.

"Liar!" he shouted at him. "'Liar', that's what they'll call you from now on. There are no mangoes in Heaven. My mother's never even seen one. I've found you out. You didn't go. You kept the money. You didn't buy your horse any food. Now he's skinny."

Iaranavi didn't answer. He went back to Ankosturaña and stayed with the Fañuru. He never saw Wanadi again. He forgot his name. Now they still call Iaranavi 'Liar' till this day, just like Wanadi called him long ago.

Now Wanadi called Hurunko. He gave him the horse without any money. He just gave him food for the journey. He told him to go to see Kumariawa.

Hurunko went. He got to Heaven. He spoke with Kumariawa. When he returned, Wanadi asked him: "How's my mother?"

"She asked about you."

"Good. Does she have food?"

"Lots of food. Yuca, jibao, pijiguao, bananas."

"Good," Wanadi answered. "You're good. You did what I asked. You told the truth. The 'Doer', that's what they'll call you now. Now I'll pay you. I won't pay Iaranavi. Punishment is the only thing he deserves."

Wanadi went to his house in the Sky, in the North, on the other side of the sea. He got shotguns, hooks, machetes, knives, shirts. He brought it all back and gave it to Hurunko. Then he started walking again. He made more houses. He made the other tribes. He made the Piaroa, the Maku, the Yabarana, the Warekena, the Haniwa, the Makushi. He made them all. He made lots of people to fight Odosha and his Fañuru.

Then he said: "Okay. I'm going to leave the Earth now. I'm going to go back to Heaven. I'm going to say goodby to my people."

WANADI NISTAMA:
Wanadi's Farewell

When Wanadi said goodby in Mawadi anehidi, he called all our grandfathers together.

He called them and gathered them around. First he spoke. Then he made a feast. They danced. They drank. They sang for three days.

"I'm going," he said. "I'm going back to Heaven. I can't live here anymore. Odosha has made himself master of the Earth. There's fighting, war, sickness, death, every kind of evil.

"I'm going. I'll be back soon. Odosha will die. When Odosha dies, the Earth will end. Then there will be another one, a good one. The sun, the moon, the stars are all going to fall on the Earth. This sky is going to fall. It's a bad sky, a fake one. Then you'll see the good Sky (Heaven) again, the real one, like in the beginning. When the sun falls, Wanadi's light will come back and shine. I'll return. I'll send you my new *damodede*, the new Wanadi. It will be me with another body, the Wanadi of the new Earth. I'll go find *Huehanna* in the mountain. The unborn people are waiting for me to be born.

"You'll die now, like I did in Karakaña. It won't be real. It'll only be a trick for Odosha.

"Your houses, your food, they're waiting for you in Kahuña. I'll be waiting for you there. Your bodies will die. Your *akato* will leave through the door of Heaven. They'll ask the keeper of the door, the Scissors Master, if they can pass. The good ones will pass. They'll climb many ladders to their houses in the Sky. The bad ones won't pass. The Scissors Master will slice them to bits in the door. They'll fall back down to Earth. They'll stay with Odosha forever. They'll die with him when the world ends.

"There are no wars in Kahuña, only peace and food and happiness. There aren't any Odoshankomo there, no sickness or disease. Life never ends. Night never comes.

"Now you'll go on living with Odosha. I'm going. I've left you the signs. I did many things to let you know. Just as I did, you'll do."

Then Wanadi spoke separately to his *Wanadi sottoi,* his twelve men from the beginning who were living with Wade in Truma achaka.

"I made a new house for my father-in-law in Kushamakari. I also made another house for you. It's hidden in the other Kushamakari. I can't take you all to Heaven. You'll stay here on Earth for now. You won't die like the others. You'll wait in the house for my return. I'm sending you to the other house, the new Kushamakari, to wait for me. It's there in front of Marahuaka, empty. The light from Heaven shines there. Odosha can't get in. I'll come for you when I return. Then I'll look for *Huehanna* and Odosha's skull."

That's how Wanadi spoke when he said goodby to the people in Mawadi anehidi. His twelve men went to the headwaters of the Kawai and Iamo at the foot of the Duida and hid in Kushamakari. They're waiting there for the end of the world.

We don't see the house, only a mountain. We can't get in to talk with those men from the beginning. There are guards hidden all along the way and a giant bat that lives in a cave on the mountain. *Huhai,* yes, they see the house as it is. They go right up to the door. They speak with the *Wanadi sottoi.* They tell them about us. They ask them for power, health, food, wisdom. They can't go in or see those people. They just speak with them through the door.

Now they began to dance. Wanadi sat down on a monkey bench in front of a *kanawa* full of *iarake.* He sang. He sang beautifully. Odosha arrived. He sat down in front of him on another bench. They both had on feathered headdresses, and bats with feathers were hanging down their backs.

When the sun rose, Wanadi was singing. He was dancing. He went away singing and dancing. Odosha was watching. He saw him. He heard him. He didn't understand.

"Here he is," he was thinking happily. But Wanadi had already gone. He had taken his *damodede* out of his body. It was empty. It was a trick. He was far away. He did it because he knew Odosha wanted to kill him. He went away first. He just left his body there. The people were dancing, drunk. Wanadi stopped singing. They couldn't see him anymore. Kaweshawa, his woman, went with him.

Now Odosha thought: "He's leaving. He's gone. I'm going too." And he ran out to catch him.

Odosha jumped in his canoe. He grabbed his paddle and chased Wanadi down the Kunukunuma. "He won't get away," he said to himself. "I'll catch him. He won't make it to Heaven."

To stop Odosha, Wanadi made fifteen rapids along the Kunukunuma. He made these fifteen rapids called Tukudi, Makuduma, Uamoatadi, Huennachadi, Amekuishodi, Mawadishodi, Hauhishodi, Wachedishodi, Huhanashodi, Schihiemenashodi, Kuttonashodi, Mahakonashodi, Kudidihanashodi, Tauatuhanashodi, and Sinashodi.

The stones in these rapids are piles of food. Wanadi cooked them and left them there for Odosha. He left an anaconda here, an agouti there, a peccary, a catfish, a frog. That was so Odosha would eat, so he would lose time. He wasn't tricked. He didn't touch any of it. He just gave it to his paddle as he rushed along behind Wanadi.

The meat was left in the river. It turned to stone. That's how the rapids came to be. They're called Agouti, Peccary, Catfish, Frog, and on and on in memory of all the food Wanadi made for Odosha.

Odosha couldn't catch him. He sent spirit animals ahead to eat him.

He sent a dog against Wanadi. The dog turned into a jaguar. Wanadi killed him with a spear. He ground up its bones and blew on them. That's how the mosquitos and gnats were born. They took off from Boca Wichada. They infested the Orinoco and swept down on Odosha. That's why there are so many mosquitos on the Orinoco.

Now Wanadi came to Maihiudi (Maipures), a little below Boca Wichada. He made his last people, the Matuto, on the rocks along the shore there. Those people turned into butterflies. They were all over the rocks. Wanadi said: "Okay. I'm going to Heaven. I'm not going to die. I'm just going to die to fool Odosha. I'm going to cut out my stomach. Odosha's coming up behind me now. He'll ask you: 'Where's Wanadi?' You answer: 'He went to Heaven.' Then he'll ask: 'Which road did he take?' You answer: 'No road. He just cut his insides out. We didn't see him again. His *akato* went off, light as a feather.'"

"Okay," said the butterflies.

Then Wanadi cut out his stomach. He threw it in the water. It's still there. It turned into stone. It's a rapids on the Orinoco now. Wanadi Nikiutahidi (Raudel del Muerto) is what we call it.

"Neumai," said the butterflies. "He's dead." Since then, we say 'Neumai' whenever a *huhai* leaves his body and takes his spirit to Heaven. Wanadi didn't return to his body. Later on, he'll come with another body. We're waiting for him to return.

Now Odosha came to Wanadi Nikiutahidi. He asked the butterflies about Wanadi.

"Here's his stomach," they said. "He went to Heaven. That's the way he did it."

"Okay," said Odosha. "I'll do that too."

He opened up his stomach and pulled out his insides. Then he looked around to see if he was in Heaven. His stomach really ached. He almost died. He ran back to look for his intestines. He stayed there a long time, recuperating, cursing Wanadi and the butterflies.

They weren't there anymore. They left right away and flew off. Those people are the last ones Wanadi made. Now they're called Colombians. They're good, rich people. They helped Wanadi against Odosha. They always come to look for us to work wood and rubber in the jungle. They pay us well. They're our friends.

Now Wanadi went down river. He came to the Cataniapo. When he cut out his stomach, he took a new body. He had the power to do that. Odosha didn't.

He sat down on his shaman's bench with Kaweshawa beside him. He smoked. He dreamt. He dreamt: "Clear water, clear, clear water." That's the way he made the Cataniapo, crystal clear and beautiful. On the shore he made a tree called *Akuhua* (Virola). Now that tree grows on the Cataniapo. He made a powder from *Akuhua*. He inhaled it through his nose. He went away, dreaming. Dreaming, he left our Earth with Kaweshawa. Their path was the clear water. They went under the Cataniapo. They arrived in Heaven. They're still living there together in peace.

Now the *Akuhua* tree stayed here for the *huhai*. They inhale it through their noses. They dream about Heaven. They travel up to the Sky the way Wanadi did. They see the invisible world.

Odosha stayed behind on Earth, cursing. When he was better, he said: "Okay. Now I'm going to find him. Now I'm going to Heaven." He got bird wings and flew off like a bird. He went flying through the clouds, beneath the sun and the moon. He flew over Ankosturaña. He flew over Karakaña. He flew everywhere looking for Wanadi. "I'm in Heaven," he thought. He was in the Earth's Heaven, the bad Heaven. He didn't know there was another Heaven. He couldn't get there. And that's the way he was fooled. He didn't find Wanadi. He's still going around looking for him. That's what the old ones say.

THE WAITIE

The Waitie were the *so'to's* first chiefs, their *kahitana*. They commanded the people. They were powerful men. They taught us how to travel on the rivers and trade. They extended our grandfathers' lands and discovered Amenadiña, the land of iron and Hurunko.

The Waitie came from the Huhai, the *so'to's* old shamans. Before the Waitie, the Huhai commanded. There were six Huhai: three Medatia from the first Medatia, then three Wasaha. Wanadi left them here when he said goodby. He left them to cure the people, to protect them from Odosha. When the third Wasaha died, he made his son the chief. His name was Kahina Waitie. This one didn't want to be a *huhai*. He just wanted to be a man. He was the chief of the people. And so the Huhai's line ended and the Waitie time began. When Kahina Waitie died, he made his son the *so'to's* chief. His name was Kaihudu. When Kaihudu died, his son became chief. His name was Iahena. Iahena had three sons: Mehudi, Tonoro, and Mahamo. They discovered Amenadiña. They brought the iron to the *so'to*. But they were never *kahitana*. A Kanaima got hold of them and drove them crazy. Iahena Waitie was the last of that line.

When the Waitie came, our grandfathers were all living in the first land called Ihuruña, in the headwaters of the Arahame, Kuntinama, and Fhadamu. That's where Wanadi made the first house for Wahnatu. Later on, Wahnatu's sons and grandchildren made other houses in Ihuruña. Each one had its own name: Kastaña, Anakadiña, Fheneña, Wasaraña, Arautaña, Kawadisokaña and others, lots of others. The old land was filled with houses. Those people were called Ihuruhana, the Headwater People. They just went on growing, making more and more houses and *conucos*. They didn't move from Ihuruña. They

165

didn't know how to make canoes. They didn't go on the rivers. They didn't know the other people, the other lands, until Iaranavi came to Ihuruña. That's how our grandfathers found out about iron and *arakusa,* about machetes and knives and the white man's shirts. They went to Ankosturaña to see Iaranavi's village and began to trade. Then the Fañuru came and took Ankosturaña. They were Odosha's people. They weren't Wanadi's. They chased Wanadi. They forced him to leave the Earth. Odosha and his Fañuru put an end to everything. Our grandfathers couldn't go to Ankosturaña anymore. There was no more trading now. They were poor again like in the beginning. No iron, no *arakusa,* just stone axes to cut down their *conucos.*

That's why Kahina Waitie gathered all the people together when he became chief. "We're all over each other here. There's no place left in Ihuruña to put any more houses or *conucos.* We'll make canoes and go down river. We'll see how it is where the other people live."

"Good," said our grandfathers. They made canoes and split up in groups to go off and explore. The young ones went. The old ones stayed in Ihuruña to watch the land. The first to go were called Yekuhana. They went east and north, down river to where the Winao (Guinau) people lived. They made their houses and *conucos* next to the Winao's. They went down the Emekuni, the Merevari, the Kanarakuni, and the Caura. Some crossed over Mount Fakudi hidi and went down the Kaimakuni and the Arakasa. Then they came to the Farimi (Uraricoera) and settled there.

Other people called Kunuhana went south. They went down the Fhadamu (Padamo) and Kunu (Kunukunuma) rivers. They made lots of houses there.

Kahina Waitie was with all of them, in all the houses. He went to Katisimaña with the Yekuhana. Then he went to the Farimi. Then he said: "I'm going to go further east."

"We'll go with you," said the Yekuhana. They went down river with him to conquer more land. That's when they learned how to pass through the rapids, when they were in the east.

When they came to Kurekurema Rapids, Shirishana were waiting for them with arrows. They were Odosha's people. They weren't Wanadi's. Our grandfathers fought the Shirishana at Kurekurema. It was the first war. They killed lots of Shirishana. They ran off in the mountains screaming like howler monkeys: "Auuu . . . auuu . . . auuu." Kahina Waitie had a house built near there called Tukuikeneña. He left some of the people there to guard the Uraricoera against the Shirisha-na people. Then he went on down river with the others to the island of Maraca. He built another house there in the mouth of the Traenida. That's where those Yekuhana stayed. They cleared the slopes of Teke-ne hidi (Mount Tepequem) and put their *conucos* there. That Traenida house was far away, on the east side. Then Kahina Waitie died and his son, Kaihudu Waitie, became chief.

When our grandfathers came to Traenida, they didn't have *sahadidi* (iron) or *arakusa* or machetes. They hadn't started trading yet. Then one day Eneiadi came to Maraca. He was one of the Ë'ti (Makushi) people. At that time, the Ë'ti lived far away, in Kanuku hidi and Ru-hunini wochi. That Ë'ti came to Maraca Island from where the sun rises. Our grandfathers looked at him. Right away, they became happy. Eneiadi was carrying a gun and a machete and some hooks. That iron was really bright. The *so'to* looked at it and touched it. They remembered Iaranavi's iron from Ankosturaña.

"Where'd you get the iron?" they asked. "Have you been in Anko-sturaña? Are you a friend of Fañuru's?"

"No," said Eneiadi. "I don't know him. Where's Ankosturaña? I just know the Matiuhana (Kariña). They have giant canoes filled with iron. They come from far away. They bring lots of iron, shotguns, shirts, everything. We trade with them. They live on the other side of Kanuku hidi, on the Ruhunini (Rupununi). That's where their villages are."

Our grandfathers offered to trade Eneiadi for his iron. "We're river people," they said. "We know how to make canoes like the Matiuha-na. If you give us the iron, we'll make you a canoe."

Eneiadi said: "You want the iron; that's why you want to make me a canoe." That's all he said.

Now they said: "We make yuca graters too. And we have hunting dogs, and *curare* for arrows. You give us the gun, the machete and the hooks and we'll give you all of that."

Eneiadi just repeated what he said before. Now they went back in the house. They told Kaihudu Waitie about Eneiadi, about the iron and the gun. Kaihudu came out of the house to see the Ë'ti man. The people all followed him. They brought all their things to show Eneiadi. They asked him to trade again. "I heard," he said. Then he didn't say anything.

Kaihudu had them prepare lots of food and *iarake* for the Ë'ti. Then they asked him to come in the house. They all got drunk together. They got drunk and sang. Now Eneiadi said: "This house and the *co-nucos* are beautiful. You give me the house and *conucos*. I'll give you the iron."

The *so'to* couldn't believe it. They didn't say anything. They just moved away from Eneiadi and began talking and whispering. Eneiadi was just standing there alone, watching from the other side. He could hear what they were saying.

Then Kaihudu came up to him. "The people don't want to leave Traenida. Our fathers came all the way from the west to build it. We were born in this house. They made these *conucos* for us. This is our land. That's why we can't leave it."

"Okay," said Eneiadi. "You don't want to give me your house. I'll keep the *arakusa*, the machete, and the hooks."

The *so'to* moved away and started talking again. They thought about it, talking like that with each other. They didn't want Eneiadi to leave with the iron. Kaihudu went to talk to the Ë'ti again. "Okay. The people have decided. We're going to leave Traenida. We'll give you the house, the *conucos,* the whole island. We're going to go back up river to where our fathers came from. We'll go back west."

Eneiadi was happy with the house. Our grandfathers kept the *arakusa*, the machete, the hooks. They shined and sparkled. They were glad to have them. But Kaihudu was sad. He wouldn't touch the iron. He called his son, Iahena Waitie. "I'm making you chief now," he said. "You move the people. You can make a new house for them up river near our brothers in Tukuikeneña."

That's why today, when a *kahitana* makes his son the chief, he moves the house. That's the custom. It began with Iahena, the third Waitie.

Our grandfathers left the east side and went back to their old lands. Iahena Waitie was their chief. As they were going up the Farimi, the Shirishana were hidden in the jungle, watching them from the shore. "They were beaten by the other people. That's why they're coming back up river." That's what the Shirishana thought. Now, right away, they attacked them to avenge their defeat by Kahina Waitie, Iahena's grandfather. The *so'to* shot the *arakusa* and frightened them. They beat them again. The Shirishana ran off into the mountains screaming and yelling. Lots of them died. The *so'to* were happy.

Then they came to Kurekurema again. They built their new house

on the shores of the Kawadi, on the slopes of Mount Kawadi hidi. Iahena Waitie called all the people together for the New House Festival.
They sang and ate and danced for five days and five nights. Then Iahena said: "Okay. We have the *arakusa*. That's why the Shirishana are
afraid. They won't attack our house. Now I want more *arakusa* to
take our brothers who stayed in the old lands. I want to take them
machetes, knives, hooks, shirts. I'm going to find the iron place. I'm
going to spy on the Matiuhana and find out where their canoes go. I'll
find out where they get the iron and *arakusa* from."

The people were happy. "We'll go with you," they said. Iahena
didn't want them to. He just wanted to take a few people, that's all.

"If we all go, the Matiuhana will see us. They'll discover us if we
have too many canoes. We won't be able to spy on them. We won't be
able to follow their canoes." That's why Iahena Waitie just called Kadahiawa. He was their *huhai*, the *so'to's* protector. He cured all the
people. He lived in the mountains near the house. Iahena Waitie called
his three sons too, Tonoro Waitie, Mehudi Waitie, and Mahamo Waitie. He also called two men who knew how to make good canoes. They
were six all together those men: four Waitie and two river men. The
seventh was Kadahiawa. He was going to protect the other six from
the Matiuhana *huhai* during their trip. The Matiuhana *huhai* were
very powerful and very evil. They turned into jaguars and attacked
people.

Then they left, the Waitie, the *huhai,* and the two men. There was a
big send-off when they left. Everyone was down on the banks of the
Farimi screaming: "Bring back lots of iron! Plenty of *arakusa!*" Then
they left and didn't come back. There was no word of them.

They were far away there, paddling, walking, then paddling again,
then walking again. When they got to the savannahs of the Ruhunini,
they saw Mount Kanuku hidi, the land of the Matiuhana. They hid in
the jungle and spied on their canoes. They saw them coming down
from the north filled with iron. Some of the canoes were being unloaded. Others were going to trade with the Ë'ti. The empty ones were
going back down the Ruhunini to get more goods.

Now Iahena said: "Let's follow them. Don't make any noise." They
got back in their canoe and followed them down the Ruhunini. They
paddled north for days. Those Matiuhana really travelled. Then they
came to the mouth of the Ruhunini and saw another, huge river. It was
called the Amenadi (Essequibo). Our grandfathers just kept following

the Matiuhana north. They followed them for days until finally, they came to the end of the Earth. They came to Dama, the Sea. It was the shore of Heaven, the shore of Lake Akuena, which is in Heaven, where only the *huhai* and spirits can enter. They found out there that the Earth ends in the north, at Dama. On the other side of Dama is Mota-dewa, Wanadi's house in Heaven. Our grandfathers discovered that, when they followed the Matiuhana people's canoes north and reached the end of the Earth.

Now they saw a village there called Amenadiña. It wasn't a *so'to* village, but a spirit village. The chief of Amenadiña was Hurunko. He was Wanadi's friend. He went to Heaven with all his people to visit Wanadi. That's why such big boats would come to Amenadiña. They'd travel across Dama and go to Wanadi's village, to Motadewa. Hurun-ko's boats would leave empty. Then they'd come back across Dama full, and unload all the goods from Heaven in Amenadiña. They'd just go and come back, go and come back.

Wanadi has huge stores in Heaven. They're filled with mountains of goods for his people. Hurunko and his people are in charge of it all. They're the only ones who can cross Dama. The Matiuhana know the secret too. They go out on Dama in their canoes but they can't cross the Sea. They can't go to Heaven because they're men. They're not spirits. They know that the iron and everything else comes from the Sky. That's why they trade with Hurunko. The Matiuhana are the ones who bring everything from Amenadiña. That's their job.

That's what Hurunko told the Waitie when they went there. He brought them into his house and fed them. The Waitie told him: "We're poor people. We come from way far away in the west, inland. We just make our canoes and *conucos,* that's all. We came to make canoes for you to trade with. But you have lots of big boats. You don't need anything from us."

Hurunko held a huge feast. He got drunk with the Waitie. Then he told them: "We're only in charge of giving the things from Heaven away. They're not ours. They're Wanadi's. We just give them to good people, to Wanadi's people. We don't give them to bad people. We don't give them to the Fañuru or the people in Ankosturaña. Now we'll give them to you since you're Wanadi's people. You can take *ara-kusa* back to your people so they can defend themselves against the Fañuru and the Shirishana. Then you'll be able to get them out of your lands. You can take Ankosturaña and give it back to Iaranavi. He's our brother.

Now Iahena Waitie went back to the *so'to* with his canoes loaded down with goods. He went to all the houses, to the Yekuhana, the Dekuhana, the Ihuruhana, the Kunuhana. They all came out to see the *arakusa* and the other treasures he'd brought from Amenadiña. They held huge feasts when he came back. That was the beginning of the feasts we have now when people come back from trading far away.

Then Iahena Waitie died. He was the last Waitie. His sons didn't become chiefs. That was the end of the Waitie, the great chiefs. Now our grandfathers didn't know the way to Kanuku hidi anymore. They sent some people out to the east to trade. They went over toward Uaiante (Auyan Tepui) and Mount Roraima. They built houses and *conucos* near the Ë'ti at the foot of Roraima and stayed there. Then some of them went north to find Amenadiña. They went up to the headwaters of the Mazaruni and built canoes. Then they paddled down river until they came to the Sea. One of them settled near Amenadiña. He was a Yekuhana named Shiriche. He didn't come back. He married one of Hurunko's women. He put his house and *conucos* there and had children. They made canoes and graters for Hurunko and got lots of iron and guns and beads. When the traders came from Roraima, they went to Shiriche's house. They just brought their things to Shiriche's house and unloaded them there.

Okay. Now we'll tell the story of Kadahiawa, the *huhai*. He was the one who brought all the bad spirits back. He went with Iahena Waitie and the others when they went to find the iron at the edge of the Sea. He went to protect them from the Matiuhana *huhai*. But he didn't protect them. He couldn't. He didn't have much power. He let the Matiuhana get him. Then he went to attack his own people. He destroyed Iahena Waitie's sons. Because of him, the Waitie came to an end. He lost all the power and wisdom of the old Huhai. Those people were left there without any protection. Then it came to the Yekuhana and Dekuhana. The people started going crazy. They started fighting with each other. The people of the lower Ventuari disappeared. The *so'to* nearly died off because of Kadahiawa. Before he came, they were everywhere. Now there are just a few.

When Iahena Waitie and his sons went to Amenadiña to get the iron from Hurunko, Kadahiawa stayed in the jungle to keep watch. He was guarding against the Matiuhana. They set Kanaima on people. Those Kanaima aren't spirits, but men. They stick the bad spirits in them. Then they let them loose in the jungle. The Kanaima take different forms. They'll come like jaguar, snakes, any animal that'll hurt you. They run around like crazy people, strangling and eating everything they see. When they look at someone, they make them crazy. Even if they escape, that look's enough to drive them crazy right away. Then they start running all over looking for other people to attack. The Kanaima just keep growing and growing. Every day there's more of them.

That's how Kanaima began with the *so'to*. Kadahiawa looked at one. He didn't know how to defend himself. He lost all his power and wisdom. He went crazy. He began running all over the mountains. Iahena Waitie's sons saw him. They turned into Kanaima and started to run. The people were afraid. Kadahiawa came to the Yekuhana houses on the Merevari and the Arakasa. Right away, the Yekuhana looked at him and went crazy. Now those Kanaima started running all over like wild animals, eating people the way Matiuhana do. The trails were all covered with human bones. Now the Kanaima ran through the Emekuni, the Kanarakuni, the Erewato, the Antawari. The *so'to* didn't have a *huhai* now. They didn't have any Waitie to defend them.

Now the Kanaima wanted to go in to where the Kaliana (Sape) live on Mount Kueki hidi. Those people hadn't lost their *huhai*. They still had plenty of power. They drove the Kanaima out. Their chief went up to Heaven, to the house of the Setawa, the maraca spirits. He got a maraca and came back down to Earth. That maraca was Medatia's. That's how the Kaliana *huhai* got Medatia's power. They drove the Kanaima out with his maraca. We call maraca Setawa Kaliana now, in memory of those people. The Kaliana kept the wisdom. Kadahiawa lost it.

The Yekuhana Kanaima ran all over. They went down to the lower Ventuari where the Dekuhana used to live. There were lots of people there then. They had no protection. There wasn't any *huhai* because of Kadahiawa. The Yekuhana came and started eating them. Then they crossed the river to where the Maku live. They had a powerful *huhai*. "How will I protect my people?" he thought. Then he sent them to get the Dekuhana's bones. They brought them back. The Maku *huhai* drove the Kanaima out with the power of those bones. The Maku weren't hurt but almost all the Dekuhana died. There aren't any of them left in the lower Ventuari now.

The *so'to* were all eating each other. Kanaima nearly killed them all. Then they thought: "What'll we do now? We don't have a *huhai*. We'll all die." Then they sent someone to the Kaliana. They asked for their protection. They helped them. That's how the Kanaima time finally ended. Later on, the Kaliana sent the *so'to* new *huhai* to protect them. That's how the *so'to* were saved.

Okay. That's everything. That's the story of the *so'to*.

Glossary

ADAHE: *Conuco.*

ADAHE ADEMI HIDI: Literally meaning 'To sing *conuco*', this is the festival for the new *conuco* held between the time of its clearing and its planting. The most important annual Makiritare festival, it lasts for from three to five days, and is the occasion for a lengthy ritual singing of many of the most important parts of the *Watunna,* the main body of which is contained in the fourteen part *Toqui.*

ADEKATO: The *akato*'s journey, which is recounted to its body in the form of dreams. The *adekato* is considered a dangerous journey, for whenever it leaves the body, the *akato* is in constant peril of being captured by Odosha.

ADEMI: *Ademi* is the most common term for 'song' and is applied to the long, ceremonial performances of the *Watunna.* When the suffix *hidi* is added, a verb form is made meaning 'to sing', as in *Adahe ademi hidi,* 'To sing *conuco'.*

ADICHAWO: The daughter of Sahatuma who is killed by her husband Momiñaru for lying to him.

AGOUTI (Akudi): *Dasyprocta aguti lunaris.* A large rabbit-sized rodent which is valued for both its meat and its teeth, the latter of which are used to make carving knives and necklaces.

AHISHA: *Casmerodius albus egrettus.* The great egret who is the double of Iaranavi in the same way that the woodpecker is the double of Wanadi. As the symbol of the white man, the egret is the master of iron.

AHISHAMA: *Icterus icterus.* The troupial, who was the first of the Star People to reach Heaven, at which time he turned into the planet Mars.

AHÖTTE: Ceremonial dance pendants hung from the biceps and made with beads, macaw and toucan feathers, animal fur or wild cotton, and small seeds which rattle as the men dance.

AICHUDI: One of the two types of sacred song (the other being *ademi*) found amongst the Makiritare, the *aichudi* are most often associated with the short-

175

er, more private 'blowing' songs used to exorcise evil spirits, expel storms, purify food, and cure the ill.

AICHUDIAHA: Literally the *'aichudi'* or 'song man', this term refers to the keeper of the *Watunna*. Neither a hereditary nor paid position, there are nevertheless in every village a small group of elders who guard and perpetuate the tradition. Although *aichudi* itself refers to the shorter, more ritually oriented songs, the *aichudiaha* is the keeper of both these and the more publicly appreciated *Watunna*. This term is synonymous with that of *ademi edamo*.

AIUKU: A hallucinogenic snuff in wide use throughout the South American rain forest, *aiuku* is variously known amongst other tribes as *ñopo, yopo,* and *vilca*. Made from the seeds of a large leguminous tree *(Anadenanthera peregrina)* which is commonly found in savanna areas, the Makiritare say that it also grows along the shore of Lake Akuena, and restrict its use to shamans.

AKATO: The body's companion spirit or double which descends from Heaven to occupy it upon birth. All *akato* are eternal, and upon the body's death the *akato* returns to live in Heaven once again. A principal cause of death is the loss of one's *akato,* which enjoys travelling at night and therefore runs the risk of being captured by Odosha.

AKENE: The deep blue water of Lake Akuena, which has the power of immortality and can restore not only the dead but also the meat of eaten animals to their bones. *Akene* is mixed with the juices of the *kaahi* plant which grows along Akuena's shores.

AKUANIYE: The peace plant which is used to make peace between warring peoples. Originally brought to Heaven by Kuamachi to make peace with the Star People, Wlaha (the Pleiades) is now the master of this plant.

AKUENA: The lake of eternal life located in Iadiñakuwa in the center of Heaven. It is an important site of passage in the shaman's initiatic journey and a favorite gathering place of the animal and plant masters, Kahuhana, and *akato,* who dwell in Heaven. Bathing in this lake immediately restores the dead to life.

AKUHUA: A hallucinogenic snuff made from the resin exuded from the thick, reddish bark of the towering *Virola calophylla* tree of the Myristicaceas family. As with *kaahi,* there are also many species of *Virola* in use amongst the rain forest tribes of South America.

AMADUWAKADI: The Morning Star. The Makiritare consider the Morning Star and the Evening Star (Kuamachi), which are both the planet Venus, to be two separate beings.

AMENADIÑA: The principal Dutch fort, located in the mouth of the Essequibo River in what is today Guyana. Amenadiña actually refers to separate locations, as the first Dutch fort, Kijkoveral, was moved from Kaow Island to Flag Island in 1738 and renamed Fort Zeelandia. The Makiritare travelled to Amenadiña to trade with the Dutch until well into the nineteenth century.

AMOAHOCHO: Having the form of a miniature yuca press (see *sebucan*), the *amoahocho* is used to squeeze out the oils of certain palm seeds. It is also used in a mating game between men and women during festivals. Working much like a Chinese finger game, when a person sticks his finger in the open end, the harder he pulls, the harder it is to escape.

ANKOSTURAÑA: Ankostura, originally the home of Iaranavi and later conquered by the Fañuru. One of the earliest Spanish settlements on the Orinoco (founded 1764), its name was changed to its present Ciudad Bolivar in 1866.

ANTAWARI: The Ventuari River. A tributary of the Orinoco whose headwaters form part of Ihuruña.

ARAHAME: A river in the headwaters of the Kuntinama, forming part of Ihuruña, the most sacred ancestral territory of the Makiritare.

ARAKUSA: A corruption of the Spanish *arcabuz* which were the old arquebusses or blunderbusses brought by the Spanish Conquistadors; this word has remained the Makiritare term for any rifle or gun. It is also the name of Kasenadu's mythical 'lightning cane'.

ATTA: The communal roundhouse, which is considered to be a replica of the universe. Because the entire village lives within a single *atta*, the terms 'house' and 'village' are interchangeable within the tales.

ATTA ADEMI HIDI: Literally 'To sing house', this is the festival held at the completion of a new *atta*. Lasting several days, the *Watunna* recounting the construction of the first house by Wanadi is sung, and all evil spirits are exorcised.

ATTAWANADI: The third *damodede* of Wanadi to be sent to the Earth, 'House Wanadi' constructed the first houses, created the first people, and taught the Makiritare many of their most important ritual and material skills.

AYADI: *Barbasco.*

BARBASCO (Ayadi): Any of a variety of vines (*Lonchocarpus sericeus, Piscidia guaricensis,* etc.) which is beaten and released into the rivers where it destroys the water's oxygen content, stunning the fish and making them float to the surface. Because of the destructiveness of *barbasco* fishing, there are tribal taboos restricting its use in any given area to not more than once a year. Attawanadi was the first to introduce *barbasco* when he used it to destroy the piranha in Kaweshawa's vagina.

BIJAO: *Heliconia bihai.* Related to the banana in the Musaceas family, this plant bears an edible fruit as well as leaves used for roofing.

CARUTO (Tununu): *Genipa americana.* A black vegetal oil derived from the tree of the same name, and used for body and facial paint.

CASSAVA (U): The large flat bread made from the root tubers of the bitter yuca plant which serves as the staple diet of the Makiritare.

CHAKARA: The shaman's medicine pouch in which he stores a variety of magic plants and herbs, tobacco, and power stones. No larger than 6" by 12", it is made from either jaguar or monkey skin, and has a strap attached so its owner can carry it across his shoulder.

CHIRIPA (Wiha): The common Spanish name for a small, beetle-like insect related to the cockroach but much quicker and only a quarter of its size.

COATI (Esheu): *Nasua solitaria*. A small South American omnivore with a long, slender tail and flexible snout. It was Coati who cleared the piranha out of Kaweshawa's vagina, a story which has led to a widely held belief in his great potency. The coati's hip bone, ground and mixed with whatever liquid, is claimed to be the most powerful aphrodisiac known.

CONUCO (Adahe): The large slash and burn gardens found throughout the greater Amazonian basin area. *Conuco* is the common Spanish term although its usage has actually been adopted by many Indians. Among the Makiritare, the *conucos* are cleared by the men and planted and maintained by the women. The main crop is the bitter yuca plant, but sweet yuca, bananas, pineapple, sugar cane, chili peppers, squash, sweet potato, tobacco, and gourd are also to be found.

CUCURITO (Wasai): *Maximiliana regia*. Known in English as the cokerite, this valuable palm supplies food, thatch, oil, and ritual clothing. The *Wasai yadi* or Festival of the Cokerite Palm is celebrated upon the return of a trading or hunting expedition which has been away from the village for an extended period of time.

CURARE: A common term for a variety of hunting poisons found amongst most lowland South American Indians. Used to tip arrows and blowgun darts, the Makiritare obtain their *curare* in trade with the Pairoa and Maku. The poison itself is a mixture of *Strychnos* plants and frog poisons.

DAMA: The Sea, which surrounds the entire Earth and is connected to Lake Akuena in the center of Heaven by underground rivers. Dama originally came to Earth as a great flood caused by Iureke and Shikiemona.

DAMODEDE: A spirit messenger or double which is conceived of as an *akato* that can be controlled and directed, a power which only *huhai* and Wanadi himself are capable of.

DARICHE: *Streptoprocne zonaris*. The white-collared swift who went to Lake Akuena to bring the first water (the Old Water) down to Earth.

DEDE: *Noctilio leporinus*. The fisher bat, Dede is also the name used by the Makiritare to refer to bats in general.

DEKUHANA (Dekuana): The name of the mountain the first Makiritare were said to have come out of, as well as the name of one of the four tribal divisions. The Dekuhana as a group lived on the lower Ventuari where they were severely decimated by their Yekuhana brothers who had been turned into Kanaima.

DEWAKA: The name of an unidentified tree and the edible fruit it bears.

DIHUKU: A small freshwater fish, known as a 'sardine' in Spanish, which although extremely boney, is still valued as food by the Makiritare. Dihuku was the first fish to swallow and nurture Kuamachi.

DINOSHI: *Harpia harpyja*. The world's most powerful eagle, the Harpy of the *Watunna* are viewed as supernatural monsters of even greater proportions. Some versions of the Dinoshi tale view them as having one enormous body and two heads, rather than as two separate birds.

DODOIMA: Mount Roraima.

DUIDA: A large table-top mountain on the southern side of the Kushamakari-Marahuaka-Duida chain. It is approximately 7,900 feet high and overlooks the Kunukunuma to the west and La Esmeralda and the Orinoco to the south.

EDENAWADI: The woman sent to Roraima by Kamaso to bring the first yuca back to the *so'to*.

EKUAI: Moriche.

'ELBOWS ON HIS KNEES, HEAD IN HIS HANDS . . .': The formula used to describe the shaman's traditional posture; this is said to be the eternal position of the great shaman masters dwelling in Heaven, the Setawa Kaliana. It is also the posture of the two figures carved back to back on the handle of the shaman's maraca.

ENEIADI: The Makushi Indian who traded iron and *arakusa* to the Yekuhana for the Island of Maraca.

ENNEKU: *Lachesis mutus*. The bushmaster who was one of the first four poisonous snakes to come down to the Earth to guard Kasenadu's *conuco*. Enneku was also the wife of Kasenadu and was subsequently devoured by the Dinoshi.

ESHEU: Coati.

Ė'TI: Makushi.

EWITI: Peak, as in Kadiio ewiti, 'Squirrel Peak'.

FADRE: A slight corruption of the Spanish *padre*, 'father' or 'priest', this was the Makiritare name given to the Capuchin missionaries who arrived with the Fañuru.

FAÑURU: A race of evil white men created by Wanadi and led astray by Odosha; the word *Fañuru* derives from the Carib *Pañoro* which in turn derives from *Español*, or 'Spanish'.

FARIMI: The Parima or Uraricoera River which flows from northern Brazil near Ihuruña due east until it enters the Rio Branco close to present-day Boa Vista.

FHADAMU: The Padamo River which flows into the Orinoco east of La Esmeralda.

FIAROANKOMO: Piaroa.

FICHA: *Piaya cayana.* The squirrel cuckoo who was responsible for losing *Huehanna.*

FRIMENE: Nuna's sister who stole *Huehanna* and later turned into Huiio. This was the first woman that Wanadi unsuccessfully courted.

HANA (also *Ana*): A suffix meaning 'people', as in *Kahuhana,* 'Heaven *(Kahu)* people'.

HIDI: Mountain, as in *Wana hidi,* 'Mount Wana'. There is another *hidi* which should not be confused with this, which serves as an auxiliary verb form when added to a noun, such as *aremi* (song) *hidi,* 'to sing'.

HÖHÖTTU: *Glaucidium brasilianum phalaenoides.* The ferruginous pygmy owl who lives in the sixth Heaven with Müdo and Tawadi and along with them forms the trinity of great shaman's helpers.

HUASA: The Makiritare term for 'brother-in-law', *huasa* is also commonly used in a more general sense to mean 'friend' or 'partner'.

HUEHANNA: The stone-like egg in which Wanadi sent his unborn people down to Earth.

HUENNA: *Tinamus tao.* The grey tinamou who meets and abandons Makusani in the forest. The tinamou's eggs are renowned for their beauty and not only does Frimene compare *Huehanna* to one, but they are also the sole containers from which *kaahi* is drunk in Heaven.

HUHAI (pronounced Fhufhai): The shaman or medicine man who is responsible for the health and well-being of his village. He cures and defends against enemy shamans and Odoshankomo, rescues kidnapped *akato,* assesses and revenges all deaths, and controls the game. The first human *huhai* was Medatia, who began the line of Huhai which served as the *so'to*'s first chiefs. The *huhai* of today are said to be considerably less powerful than these first great shaman chiefs.

HUHAI'S BENCH (Müde): One of the *huhai*'s most important objects is his magic bench, a low, wooden seat carved in either the form of a jaguar or a monkey. It is with this bench that the *huhai* is transported to Heaven.

HUIIO: A supernatural anaconda many times larger than any visible one, Huiio is the mistress of all water and the mother of everything living in it.

Quite literally the 'Plumed Serpent', she wears the feathered rainbow and lives under the rapids with her *mawadi* people.

HURUNKO: A race of good white people created by Wanadi in the mouth of the Essequibo River, these were the Dutch who occupied Guyana until 1814, when it was ceded to Great Britain.

IAHENA WAITIE: The third and last of the great Waitie chiefs who discovered Amenadiña and brought back iron.

IAHI: *Psophia crepitans*. The gray-winged trumpeter who was sent to kill the Dinoshi.

IAMANKAVE: The mistress of yuca from whom Kuchi stole the first yuca to be planted on the Earth.

IAMO: Originating in Mount Marahuaka where it creates a large falls, this river is a tributary of the Kunukunuma.

IARAKARU: *Cebus apella fatuellus*. The weeping capuchin monkey who was Wanadi's nephew and let the night out of his *chakara*.

IARAKE: The most important alcoholic beverage of the Makiritare, made with fermented bitter yuca and the leaves of a certain tree.

IARANAVI: The first white men created by Wanadi in San Fernando de Atabapo, forced by the Fañuru to move to Ankostura, where they traded with the Makiritare until the Fañuru finally conquered them and made them their servants.

IARURUKO: *Tupinambis nigropunctatus*. An enormous, forked tongued water lizard who was one of the animals to kill and eat Kuamachi's mother.

IAWA: *Cichla ocellaris*. Known in English as the peacock bass because of the large black spot on its tail, this was the second fish to swallow and incubate Kuamachi.

IHETTE: One Leg, who was named that because the caiman cut off his leg before he fled into the sky with Wlaha and the other Star People to become Orion's Belt.

IHURUHANA: The Headwater (*Ihuruña*) people (*hana*), who are one of the four tribal divisions of the Makiritare, occupying the tribe's ancestral headwater territory.

IHURUÑA: The Headwater Place, so named because of its location at the headwaters of a group of rivers which include the Padamo, Kuntinama, Erebato, Ventuari, Arahame, and Caura. This large area of savannas and mountains is said to have been the original site of the first Makiritare and is still respected as their most sacred territory. Mount Dekuhana, Wana hidi, and Kamaso wochi are all located within this area.

IOROKO: The name of a demon who tried to climb to Heaven on Wlaha's ladder, *Ioroko* is actually a borrowing of the Kariña word for Odosha.

IUKUTA (also Sukutaka): The principal Makiritare beverage made from cassava and water and drunk in great quantities at every meal.

IUMAKAWA: Kuchi's sister, who lives in Heaven and saved his life after he had been skinned by Iamankave. Other versions of this story identify her as a paca and say that she made his new skin out of tobacco leaves.

IUREKE: The younger of the twin heroes who came out of *Huehanna,* Iureke is the trickster par excellence and as a result is one of the most popular mythic characters among the Makiritare.

IYAKO: *Paraponera.* Known as the *veinticuatro* or 'twenty-four hour' ant because of intense fever one receives from its bite, this is one of the most feared insects in all of South America.

KAAHI: A hallucinogenic made from a Malphighiaceous vine of the genus *Banisteriopsis* (there are various species), which is prepared and taken in liquid form. As with *aiuku* and *akuhua,* the use of *kaahi* amongst the Makiritare is restricted to the *huhai* who uses it to travel to Heaven and make contact with the invisible world. Closely related to the word for Heaven, *Kahu, kaahi* is its equivalent, growing at its center beside Lake Akuena and mixing with its waters. One of the most widespread hallucinogens among the native peoples of South America, it is also known as *caapi, yage,* and in Ecuador as *ayahuasca,* the 'dead man's vine'.

KADAHIAWA: The *huhai* who went to Amenadiña with Iahena Waitie and turned into a Kanaima. It was Kadahiawa who lost the power of the old Huhai and began the decimation of the *so'to.*

KADAU: *Daptrius americanus.* The red-throated caracara who served as Mahanama's guard.

KADIIO: *Guerlinguetus aestuans.* The squirrel whose home is located on the top of the Duida in *Kadiio ewiti.*

KAHINA WAITIE: The first of the great Waitie chiefs who led the Yekuhana to their most easterly expansion on the Uraricoera.

KAHITANA: Chief. Although the first Waitie chiefs were pan-tribal and hereditary, the present-day chiefs are chosen at will by their village and do not command beyond them. Chiefs may also be *huhai* but this is not common.

KAHIURU: The chief of the Fañuru who was Odosha's *damodede* sent by him to head the Fañuru and fight against Wanadi.

KAHIUWAI: *Anhinga anhinga.* The anhinga who was created from one of Frimene's gourds as she fled Nuna's house. Although only briefly mentioned here, it appears that the anhinga, a bird that dives under water to catch its food, was actually a transitional stage in the transformation of Frimene into Huiio.

KAHSHE: *Serrasalmus spp.; Pygocentrus spp.* The piranha or 'cannibal' fish, notorious for its sharp teeth and ability to cut through anything.

KAHU: Heaven or Sky. See Kahuña.

KAHU (also Kahushawa): Other names for Odosha, the master of all evil. Kahu, which is strongly accented on the first syllable, should not be confused with Kahu (Heaven) which is accented on the last.

KAHUAKADI: The master of blowgun cane *(kurata)* who lives on Tahashiho Peak on Mount Marahuaka where the blowgun cane grows. Kahuakadi originally went to live on Tahashiho after fighting with his miserly sister, Arüwo, who wouldn't share her cassava with him.

KAHUHANA: The Heaven or Sky People who live in Kahuña.

KAHUÑA: Heaven or the 'Sky Place', conceived of as being divided into eight separate villages or lands, each one inhabited by a different family of powerful *huhai*. The *huhai* initiate must travel to Heaven to visit all these houses (with the exception of the eighth which only Wanadi enters) and receive his various powers — maraca, *wiriki*, companion spirits, etc., from them. Kahuña is guarded by the Scissors Master who prevents any Odoshankomo or demons from entering.

KAICHAMA: Momiñaru's reincarnated form with which he returns to Earth to avenge himself on Sahatuma. The name Kaichama is no doubt a variant of 'Kachimana', the plant spirit who 'makes fruits ripen' and is called by the use of ritual flutes or *momi*.

KAIHUDU WAITIE: The second of the great Waitie chiefs, who traded the Island of Maraca for a shotgun, a machete, and some hooks.

KALIANA (Sape): A small, linguistically independent tribe living in the headwaters of the Paragua River. They are highly respected by the Makiritare for the great power of their shamans.

KAMASO: The chief who had the first yuca brought from Mount Roraima. His village in Kamaso wochi (Kamaso's Savanna) in the headwaters of the Arahame is considered the heart of Ihuruña and is said to be the first place Wanadi set foot on Earth.

KANAIMA: A highly feared form of black magic widespread throughout the Carib-speaking Indians of eastern Venezuela and Guyana. The Yekuhana brought back Kanaima when they went to Amenadiña to find iron. Versions vary as to what a Kanaima actually is, but most agree that it is a person turned into a monster, jaguar, snake, etc., who ruthlessly kills for revenge, hire, or just the pleasure of it.

KANAWA: A large, hollowed-out log used in the preparation and drinking of *iarake*. The inauguration of a new *kanawa* is the occasion of an important festival known as *Kanawa awidi,* 'Carving the Kanawa'.

KARAKAÑA: Caracas, which was built by Wanadi and then occupied by the Fañuru.

KARAKARADI: *Sarcoramphus papa.* The king vulture who gave Jaguar his eyes.

KARIÑA (Matiuhana): Most commonly known by their Arawak name, Carib, this was the single largest tribe east of the Andes at the time of the Conquest. Greatly feared by their neighbors as cannibals and slave traders, the Kariña became close allies of the Dutch in their two hundred and fifty year long war with the Spanish invaders.

KASENADU: Lightning Man, who terrorized the people with his 'Lightning Cane' *(Arakusa)* until he was vanquished by his nephew, Wachamadi.

KASUWARAHA: *Tupinambis teguixin.* The enormous tegu lizard who is Wanadi's brother-in-law and most important companion spirit.

KAWAO: *Pipa americana.* This toad was the first mistress of fire but had it taken away from her by Iureke and Shikiemona, the twin heroes whom she adopted.

KAWESHAWA: Wanadi's wife as well as the daughter of the master of fish whose name is in Kasuruña Rapids.

KOMO: A suffix meaning 'people', as in Fiaroankomo, 'Fiaroa people'.

KÖ NNÖ TÖ : *Bothrops atrox.* The fer-de-lance, which was one of the first four poisonous snakes sent down to Earth in order to guard Kasenadu's *conuco*.

KONOTO: *Psarocolius decumanus.* Known as yellowtails because of their long tailfeathers of the same color, the crested *oropendola* travel in large, noisy flocks and are often to be found around *conucos*.

KRUZA AKE: The Cross, from the Spanish *cruz*.

KUAMACHI: Venus, or more accurately Vesper, the Evening Star, as distinguished from Amaduwakadi, the Morning Star. It was Kuamachi who drove Wlaha and his Shiriche (Stars) into the sky in an attempt to avenge his mother.

KUCHI: *Potos flavus chapadensis.* Related to the coati, the kinkajou is a tree-dwelling omnivore with enormous eyes and a long, coiled tail, used to hang from branches during the night. It was Kuchi who went to Heaven to steal the first yuca.

KUDENE: The anaconda man who made the first *curare* in order to kill the Dinoshi monsters.

KUDEWA: *Amazona amazonica.* The orange-winged parrot who watched over Kumariawa's grave and called to Wanadi when she appeared.

KUDI: The tree Kasenadu stuck the hearts of the Dinoshi in. It subsequently turned into a mountain of the same name, which is located in the headwaters of the Ventuari.

KUINADI: *Trogon collaris*. The collared trogon which is related to the quetzal and the master of the *moriche* palm.

KUMARIAWA: Wanadi's mother whom he created himself in order to kill and restore to life in an attempt to show the illusion of death and thus discredit Odosha.

KUMNUATTE: One of the two trees the twin heroes hid the first fire in, giving origin to its use as a fire drill.

KUNU: The Kunukunuma River, which flows into the Orinoco between the Casiquiare and La Esmeralda.

KUNUHANA: 'People of the Kunu'. One of the four tribal divisions of the Makiritare, the Kunuhana live along the Kunukunuma and Padamo Rivers.

KURAHUA: *Bromelia fastuosa*. A species of *Bromelia* from which string, rope, fishing line, and other products are made.

KURATA: *Arthrostylidium schomburgkii*. A long, very straight bamboo which is only found within the Makiritare's borders, *kurata* is used to make the blowguns of the same name. Because of the Makiritare monopoly on this cane, the blowgun has become a very important trade item for them.

KURUMANKOMO: The race of black people who arrived with the Fañuru.

KURUNKUMO: The curassow who lives in Fauhi ewiti (Curassow Peak) and kidnapped Kaweshawa, Kurunkumo is the bird spirit of Odosha.

KUSHAMAKARI: Literally meaning the *hamakari* or 'house' of Kushi (Kuchi), this was the site of Wanadi's home on the Earth. A tall, table-top mountain in the upper Kunukunuma, Wanadi was supposedly so enamored with its beauty that he moved his original home there from Ihuruña. It is this mountain which is said to be the center post of the universe, holding up the Heavens.

KUTTO: *Hyla spp*. This frog was the first to reach the sky with Ahishama, where he turned into an unidentified constellation.

MADI: The white kaolin clay with which Wanadi tried to make a woman to replace Kaweshawa, and later used again to make Iaranavi and Hurunko. Also the name of an unidentified tree bearing edible fruit.

MADO: *Panthera onca*. The jaguar, which is the form most commonly taken by shamans to carry out their tasks on Earth. This is one of the few animals that is said to have been specifically created by Wanadi himself.

MADUNAWA: The first *so'to* woman to successfully plant yuca.

MAHAIWADI: A powerful shaman who defeated the Fañuru in what appears to be a memory of the Makiritare rebellion against the Spanish in 1775.

MAHAMO WAITIE: One of Iahena Waitie's three sons driven crazy by Kanaima.

MAHANAMA: Kuamachi's grandfather, whom some storytellers say was the father-in-law of Wanadi.

MAHEWA: The blue morpho butterfly who is the master of Lake Akuena.

MAKAKO: A small lizard who serves Odosha in much the same way that Kasuwaraha serves Wanadi.

MAKU: A small tribe of Saliva-speaking Indians closely related to the Piaroa, who live around the lower Ventuari River.

MAKUSANI: The boy who travels to the house of the moon and the house of the sun. The name Makusani is closely related to that of the Kariña and Makushi culture hero, Makunaima, 'the one who works in the dark', and no doubt has its origins amongst these peoples.

MAKUSHI (Ė'TI): A Cariban-speaking tribe living between the Cotinga and upper Rupununi around the area of the Kanuku Mountains in Guyana. The Makiritare consider them to be highly dangerous Kanaima masters.

MAMAKU: An evil shaman who lived on Mount Guanayo on the upper Orinoco. The Shirishana ate him and subsequently went crazy.

MAMURE: *Anthurium flexuosum*. A large, flexible vine used as cord or rope.

MANARE: The large flat strainers used by the Makiritare in the preparation of their cassava.

MANI: Peraman.

MANIOC (Mañoco): A toasted farina, made from the root tubers of the bitter yuca plant, which can be stored for long periods and eaten straight or with water.

MANUWA: The jaguar who was married to Kawao and raised the twin heroes. He was the first one to eat meat.

MARACA: The shaman's gourd rattle whose great magical properties are attributed to the *wiriki* crystals inside it. The maraca, the first of which was created by Wanadi, is used in virtually all shamanic activities.

MARAHUAKA: An 8,500-foot mountain located in the valleys between the Padamo and Kunukunuma Rivers. The tallest mountain in Venezuelan Guayana, Marahuaka ('Little Gourd') is the petrified memory of the first yuca tree of the same name.

MARAKUHAÑA: San Fernando de Atabapo, which is said to be the birthplace of both the Puinave and Iaranavi. Located at the mouth of the Atabapo, San Fernando was one of the first Spanish settlements on the Orinoco.

MARRIAGE: Endogamous and matrilocal, men enter the households of their fathers-in-law, accepting their authority in what is often referred to in the *Watunna* as 'marriage service'. Polygamy is not uncommon and men are often married to sisters.

MARIMA: A tree yielding a white latex which Wanadi discovered in his flight from Kurunkumo.

MATIUHANA: Kariña.

MATUTO: Except for Mahewa, the blue morpho, the Makiritare do not distinguish between butterflies, and refer to them all as Matuto, claiming it is the same insect continually painting itself with different designs. As a reward for helping Wanadi against Odosha, the Matuto were turned into the Colombians.

MAWADI: Enormous, supernatural anacondas who live under the rapids with their mistress, Huiio. They are very feared for their habit of kidnapping women and turning over canoes, as well as for their ability to cause floods.

MAWADI ANEHIDI: The rapids on the Kunkunuma where Wanadi said farewell to the *so'to*. Literally meaning 'Cooking Mawadi', it was where Wanadi killed a giant *mawadi* and cooked it to leave for Odosha.

MEDATIA: The shamanic prototype, Medatia was the first human *huhai* after Wanadi, and began the line of Huhai who originally ruled the *so'to*.

MEDIKIU: A vegetal salt made from the ashes of various palm leaves, amongst them the *moriche, cucurito,* and *chiquichiqui (Leopoldinia piassaba)*.

MEHUDI WAITIE: One of Iahena Waitie's three sons, driven crazy by Kanaima.

MEKURU: The grandfather of the Kurumankomo (Black people) who came as Kahiuru's servant.

MERARAÑA: La Esmeralda (also Esmeraldas), a Spanish settlement founded in 1760 by Apolinar Diaz de la Fuente between the mouths of the Kunukunuma and Padamo Rivers on the Upper Orinoco.

MOMI: A fibrous bark used to make ritual horns often referred to by the same name.

MOMIÑARU: The brother of Kasenadu who killed Sahatuma, thereby giving birth to the first jaguar.

MÖNETTA: The scorpion, which forms the Ursa Major.

MORICHE (Ekuai): *Mauritia Minor*. Referred to by the Warau Indians as the 'Tree of Life', this highly valued palm yields food, shelter and weaving materials, and an ash which is said to give superhuman strength.

MOTADEWA: The shamanic or secret name for Heaven (Kahuña) in general, as well the name specifically given to Wanadi's village there, which is often described as the impenetrable eighth Heaven.

MOTTODONA: The bumblebee.

MÜDO: *Nyctibius grandis*. The great potoo who is Wanadi's brother and one of the three great bird spirits living in the sixth Heaven, Matawahuña. Despite his position as one of the most powerful shaman helpers, Müdo is often made fun of because of his ugliness.

MURUNMATTO: Mestizo, people of mixed white, black, and Indian blood.

ÑA: A suffix denoting place or village, such as Amenadiña, 'the Amenadi village', or Kahuña, 'the Heaven' or 'Sky Place'.

NADEIUMADI: Wanadi's second *damodede*, who returned to Heaven after Odosha killed his mother, Kumariawa.

NAMARU: *Potamotrygon motoro*. The stingray, which was the third fish to swallow and incubate Kuamachi.

NAÑUDI: *Pteronura brasiliensis*. The great otter or nutria which grows up to six feet long, and is to be found throughout South America.

NEUMAI: Translated as 'he's dead', this is the traditional call made by the shaman when an initiate collapses under his first dosage of drugs and begins his journey to Kahuña. It is very possible that the name Nadeiumadi is derived from it.

NIGUAS (Sicha): *Tunga penetrans*. A small species of jigger which burrows under the skin and nails where it lays its eggs, thus causing a throbbing pain and itching. They are most often removed with a needle.

NONO: Earth.

NUNA: The moon, who is an evil cannibal who spends all his time trying to catch *akato* and *huhai* travelling between Earth and Heaven. It is said that when the moon has a ring around it, Nuna is about to eat someone and a shaman must go up to rescue them.

ÑOMO: The snake mistress who captures the *akato* of those bitten by her poisonous children by making them drink a beverage of forgetfulness which she claims is *iukuta*.

ODOMA: Paca.

ODOSHA: Also known as Kahu and Kahushawa, Odosha is the master of evil and the incarnation of all negative forces in the universe. Born from Seruhe Ianadi's placenta, Odosha lives with his Odoshankomo in dark caves in a land called Koiohiña and is involved in a constant struggle to dominate the Earth.

ODOSHANKOMO: Odosha's people, the demons or evil spirits.

ONOTO: Wishu.

P: The Makiritare language does not have a *P* sound and borrowed words such as Padre and Piaroa are converted into *F*'s, i.e., Fadre and Fiaroa.

PACA (Odoma): *Cuniculus paca.* A large tailless rodent with a short snout found in great numbers throughout the South American rain forest. Their inordinate ability to procreate has given them a reputation very similar to that of the rabbit.

PECCARY (Dukadi): *Tayassu pecari.* A wild boar which is one of the most important game animals to be found in tropical South America. This is in part due to the fact that they are the only large mammals to travel in herds, a fact which also makes these tusked animals considerably dangerous to hunt.

PENDARE: *Mimusops bidentata.* The chicle tree, referred to for the curative values Wanadi is said to have discovered in it.

PERAMAN (Mani): *Symphonia globulifera.* A tree yielding a thick, black resin of the same name which is used for a variety of purposes from plugging holes in canoes to waxing rope and gluing.

PIAROA (Fiaroa or Fiaroankomo): A Saliva-speaking tribe, of approximately the same size as the Makiritare, who live west of the lower Ventuari to the Sipapo River on the Colombian border. As providers of *curare* and *aiuku* for the Makiritare, they are highly respected for their great shamanic powers.

PIJIGUAO: *Guilielma gasipaes.* A tall, spiny-trunked palm tree which yields a highly coveted fruit.

PUINAVE (Winavi): A now nearly extinct Arawakan tribe inhabiting the Orinoco, around the mouths of the Guiviare and Atabapo Rivers.

R: The Makiritare language does not have a hard *R* sound but rather one that falls somewhere between a *D* and an *R*. This has often resulted in confusion where anthropologists and other investigators have randomly mixed the two (*R* and *D*) in making written records of the language. Words such as *Mado* and *mawadi,* for example, have often been transcribed as *Maro* and *mawari.*

RAKO RAKO: A small reed flute made from *shimadde* bamboo.

RORAIMA (Dodoima): Located at the junction of the borders of Guyana, Venezuela, and Brazil, Roraima is the largest mountain in the Guyana Highlands (9094 feet) and has been a sacred place for many different tribes for hundreds of years.

RUPUNUNI (Ruhunini): A tributary of the Essequibo River, flowing northeast from the Kanuku Mountains.

SADASHE: Every species, both plant and animal, has its own chief or master which is known as its *sadashe.* This *sadashe* is conceived of as the species' grandfather or prototype, its personal culture hero who gave it its name, form, and language.

SAHADIDI: Iron.

SAHATUMA: Said to have been created by Wanadi himself, the first jaguar, Mado, was born from Sahatuma's blood after he was killed by ants.

SAHUDIWA: *Schnella bicomata*. Known as 'vine-chain', this was what the Star People used to build their ladder to Heaven.

SAKASAKARI: *Megaceryle torquata*. The ringed kingfisher, found throughout the South American rain forest area.

SAPE: Kaliana.

SARORO: *Lutra enudris*. A smaller species of otter similar to that found in North America.

SEBUCAN (Tingkui): A long wickerwork sleeve used to squeeze out the bitter yuca's poison in the preparation of cassava and manioc.

SEDEDETIU: *Crotalus durissus terrificus*. The rattlesnake, which was one of the four poisonous snakes sent down to Earth to guard Kasenadu's *conuco*.

SEMENIA: *Campylorhamphus trochilirostris*. The red-billed scythebill, who was the chief of Wanadi's Bird People, created to cut down Marahuaka and clear the first *conuco*. Semenia is the master of the Earth's yuca, who taught the people the skills of cultivation.

SERUHE IANADI: Wanadi's first *damodede*, who returned to Heaven after Odosha was born from his placenta.

SETAWA KALIANA: The shaman masters who dwell in Iadekuma, the second Heaven. Never eating or sleeping, they spend all their time with 'their elbows on their knees and their heads in their hands' and it is their form which is carved on the handle of every shaman's maraca.

SHI: The sun, who created Wanadi by blowing on some *wiriki*. This proto-creator Shi (whose true secret name is Kamuñawana) should not be confused with the visible Shi we see in the sky.

SHIDISHIDI: The cockroach.

SHIKIEMONA: The elder of the twin heroes, portrayed as less adept and cunning than his brother Iureke.

SHIMI: The oil extracted from the *seje* palm *(Jessenia bataua)* and mixed with other pigments such as *caruto* to make face and body paints.

SHIRICHE: The stars, being both the stars we see in our own sky (Wlaha and his Star People) and the invisible stars who dwell in Shiriche Kumenadi at the top of Heaven. These invisible stars are deceased shamans, and a shooting star is therefore said to be a shaman who has just died and is returning to Heaven. 'Star' is also the term used to denote a year's time.

SHIRISHANA: A linguistically independent tribe of hunters and gatherers living in widely dispersed groups throughout southern Venezuela and northern Brazil. Traditional enemies of the Makiritare whom they disparagingly refer to as 'howler monkeys', the Shirishana are most commonly known as Yanoamo, Guaika, Sanema, or Guaharibo.

SHODI: Rapids, such as Tukudi shodi, 'Gourd Rapids'.

SIWO: A horn made from the bark of the *nikua* tree which is used to begin the *Adahe ademi hidi*. It is said that Semenia's voice is hidden inside this horn and that he made the original *siwo* to call the animals to the first *Adahe ademi hidi*.

SOSOWI: *Icterus chrysocephalus*. The *moriche* oriole who was one of the animals to kill and eat Kuamachi's mother.

SO'TO: A human being or person, defined as being a member of the Makiritare tribe and speaking their language. *So'to* is also the word for 'twenty', just as *Pemon* and *Kariña* are, in the respective languages of those tribes.

SUMUNUADI: *Dryocopus lineatus*. The lineated woodpecker who was one of the four birds to cut down the Marahuaka tree.

TAHU: Stone or rock, as in *tahuanohonato*, 'the shaman's wisdom stones', and *Sokoa tahu*, 'Sokoa Rock', a small rocky island in the mouth of the Atabapo.

TAPIR (Wachedi): *Tapirus terrestris*. The largest of all the South American land mammals, the tapir is a herbivore that moves around mainly at night and spends a large amount of its time in the water.

TAWADI: *Podager nacunda*. The nacunda nighthawk who dwells with Müdo and Höhöttu in Heaven and acts as one of the most powerful of all shaman's helpers.

T'DADEMA: *Micrurus hemprichii*. The coral snake, which was one of the first four poisonous snakes to come down to the Earth.

T'DENKE: The ritual process of fishing with *barbasco*, which is participated in by the entire village.

TEKOYE: Classified as clarinets because of their inner, adjustable reeds, these five-foot-long instruments are always played in pairs, male and female. Often referred to as *wanna*, which is the name of the bamboo they are made from, the *tekoye* are not subject to any of the strict taboos to be found among other Amazonian tribes concerning similar instruments.

TONORO: Bird, the generic name being derived from Wanadi tonoro, the Wanadi bird. Tonoro was also the name of one of Iahena Waitie's three sons.

TOROHA: A wickerwork fish trap which is constructed in the form of two concentric cones, *toroha* are tied to the shore and left untended during the night.

TOSEDE: The water hen or gallinule which is often found in marshy areas, as was the case when he met Iureke and Shikiemona after the flood.

TRAENIDA: The Traida River which runs south along Mount Tepequem and joins the Uraricoera at the Island of Maraca. This was the limit of the Makiritare's most easterly expansion under the Waitie.

TRUMA ACHAKA: The site of Wade's home at the foot of Mount Marahuaka as well as the location of the *so'to*'s first *conuco*.

TUDI: An open, wickerwork backpack carried with a bark line from either the head or the shoulders, *tudi* are used for carrying both game and cassava.

TUKUDI: A gourd, as in Tukudi shodi, 'Gourd Rapids'.

TUKUI: *Colibri coruscans*. The sparkling violetear, one of the two-hundred-and-thirty-five species of hummingbirds known to exist in South America.

TUNUNU: Caruto.

UDUDI: A hairy dwarf who serves as one of Odosha's messengers and is said to have been created by him.

URARICOERA: Farimi.

WACHAMADI: The master of Lightning and Thunder, who took them away from his uncle, Kasenadu.

WACHEDI: Tapir.

WACHEDI CHATO: Tapir's Jawbone, the name of an unidentified constellation.

WADAKANE: The crab, who also represents an unidentified constellation.

WADE: *Bradypus tridactylus*. The grandfather of the sloths (who are more commonly known as *waderata*), Wade was Wanadi's teacher and friend and the most powerful shaman from amongst the 'old people'.

WAHI: A small, hand-held, conically shaped fishnet primarily used by women when fishing with *barbasco*.

WAMEDI: The rooster, who sings '*Wanadi nistama*', 'Wanadi's gone'.

WAHNATU: The first Makiritare created by Wanadi from the clay of Mount Dekuhana.

WAIAMO: *Testudo sculpta*. The tortoise or box turtle who is a common trick-ster figure in the myths of many of the Guyana Indians.

WAITIE: The first line of great chiefs to command the Makiritare after the Huhai. It was the Waitie who led the expansion out of Ihuruña and brought the *so'to* their iron and *arakusa*.

WANADI: God, culture hero, and proto-shaman all in one, Wanadi is the unknowable, unseen force ('light') in Heaven, who since his farewell to the Earth has taken no part in the affairs of humans. Created by Shi, the sun, it was Wanadi (through his *damodedes*) who established order as it is known today amongst the *so'to*.

WANADI TONORO: *Phloeoceastes melanoleucos*. The crimson-crested woodpecker who is Wanadi's double and a form he often takes to carry out his tasks. As the great 'House-builder', it is not surprising that Wanadi should take the form of the 'carpenter bird'.

WANA HIDI: A mountain on the Upper Kuntinama where Wanadi built his first house, later moved to Kushamakari.

WANNA: The bamboo from which the *tekoye* clarinets are made. This bamboo is also stripped and used for making *waja* baskets.

WANWANNA: The word for dance in general, *Wanwanna* has also come to be synonymous with the *Adahe ademi hidi*, the prototype of all Makiritare dances.

WARAIHAI: *Campylorhamphus procurvoides*. The curve-billed scythebill who was one of the four birds to cut down the Marahuaka tree.

WAREMO: *Myrmecophaga tridactyla*. The anteater, who is not eaten by the Makiritare and is highly respected for his unusual strength.

WASAHA: The ceremonial dance stick which is beaten to begin all *Watunna* recitals. Hollowed out, with deer hooves attached to its top, the *Wasaha* is also beaten by the lead dancer and singer at festivals in order to keep the rhythm. Its name originates from the three great Wasaha Huhai who followed the Medatia in commanding the first *so'to*.

WASAI: Cucurito.

WASUDI: The rainbow, which is Huiio's feathered crown and therefore her symbol. Because of this association, the rainbow is considered a negative sign and very dangerous for women and children to look at.

WATTE: An unidentified bird whose name means 'I can't. I'll fall'. Wlaha named him this when he refused to fly after his arrows.

WEDAMA: *Atticora melanoleuca*. The black-collared swallow who is the son of Iamankavi, the yuca mistress.

WETASHI: The first Makiritare woman, created by Wanadi as a mate for Wahnatu.

WIHA: Chiripa.

WINAO (Guinau): A now extinct Arawakan tribe who formerly lived in much of the present day Makiritare territory and are believed to have been assimilated by them. Their own name was Temomöyamo.

WINAVI: Puinave.

WIRIKI: Small quartz crystals known as the 'shaman's power stones' with which Wanadi himself was created by Shi. Every shaman, during his initiation, must travel to Heaven to receive his own *wiriki* which he then puts in his maraca along with the roots of the shaman's drugs, *aiuku* and *kaahi*. When a shaman dies, his maraca remains on the Earth but his *wiriki* return to Heaven with him. Makiritare say that a long time ago, all people were created from *wiriki*.

WISHU: *Bixa orellana*. The small, bushy onoto tree from which a red body paint and dye of the same name are derived. This was also one of the two trees Iureke and Shikiemona hid the first fire in.

WIWIIO: *Dendrocygna autumnalis*. The black-bellied tree duck which was one of the two birds created by Frimene's falling gourds as she fled her brother Nuna's house. These birds are very likely part of a longer myth recounting Frimene's transition into Huiio.

WLAHA: The chief of the Shiriche, or Star People, who led them into the sky where he turned into the Pleiades along with his six *damodede*. The symbol of peace and harmony, this constellation is the most important one in determining Makiritare planting cycles.

WOMO ANSAI: Long, feathered dance pendants which are worn around the neck and hung down the back.

WUWA: The only Makiritare basket to be woven by the women, *wuwa* are used in the harvesting of yuca and gathering of firewood and carried from the head by bark thump-lines.

YABARANA: A nearly extinct Carib-speaking tribe dwelling along the Manafiari River, north of the Makiritare.

YAVI: A tall sandstone mesa located in the headwaters of the Manafiari and Parucito Rivers (both tributaries of the lower Ventuari), Mount Yavi was the site of Iureke and Shikiemona's home on the Earth. It is very curious that the twin heroes' home was not located in Makiritare territory, but in Yabarana, a fact which may indicate the foreign origin of this cycle.

YEKUHANA (Yecuana): One of the four tribal divisions of the Makiritare often used to designate the entire tribe. The name itself, Yekuhana, is believed to mean 'Canoe' or 'Water log People', from *ye*—'wood', 'log', *ku*—'water', *hana*—'people'.

YELLOWTAIL: Konoto.

YUCA: *Manihot utilissima*. The bitter yuca plant from which cassava and manioc are made, forming the staple diet of the Makiritare. A large, bushy plant from which all other food is said to have originated, the bitter yuca yields enormous tuber roots which must be grated and pressed in order to get out the poisonous prussic acid contained within them. In addition to the nine varieties of bitter yuca the Makiritare identify, they also grow a sweet yuca *(Manihot dulcis)* which is either eaten boiled or drunk in a fermented drink called *cashiri.*

Design by David Bullen
Typeset in Mergenthaler Sabon
by Robert Sibley
Printed by Maple-Vail
on acid-free paper

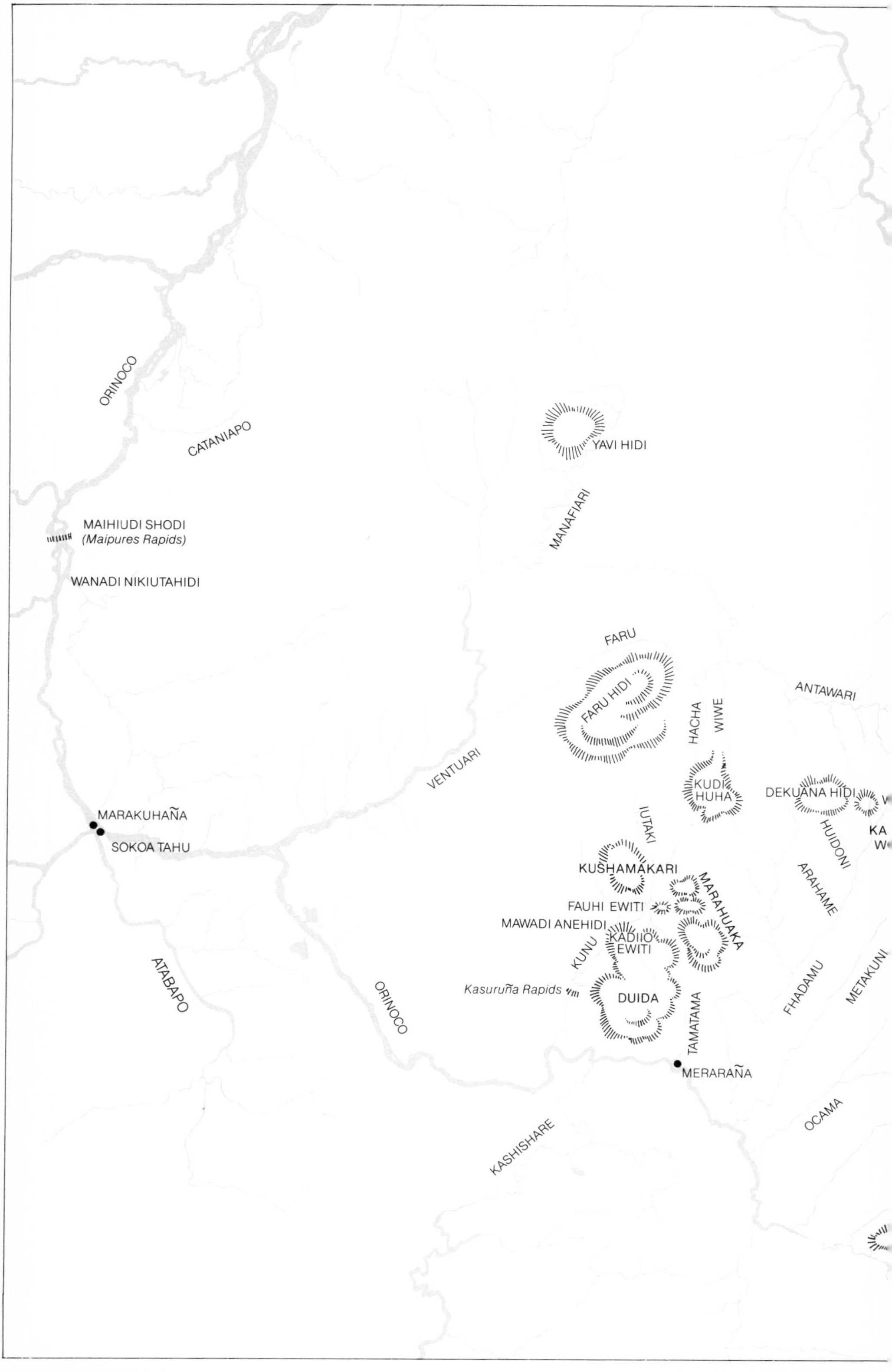

ORINOCO

CATANIAPO

YAVI HIDI

MANAFIARI

MAIHIUDI SHODI
(Maipures Rapids)

WANADI NIKIUTAHIDI

FARU

FARU HIDI

HACHA
WIWE

ANTAWARI

VENTUARI

KUDI
HUHA

DEKUANA HIDI

KA
W

MARAKUHAÑA

SOKOA TAHU

IUTAKI

KUSHAMAKARI

HUIDONI

ARAHAME

MARAHUAKA

FAUHI EWITI

MAWADI ANEHIDI

KUNU

KADIIO
EWITI

FHADAMU

METAKUNI

ATABAPO

ORINOCO

Kasuruña Rapids

DUIDA

TAMATAMA

MERARAÑA

OCAMA

KASHISHARE

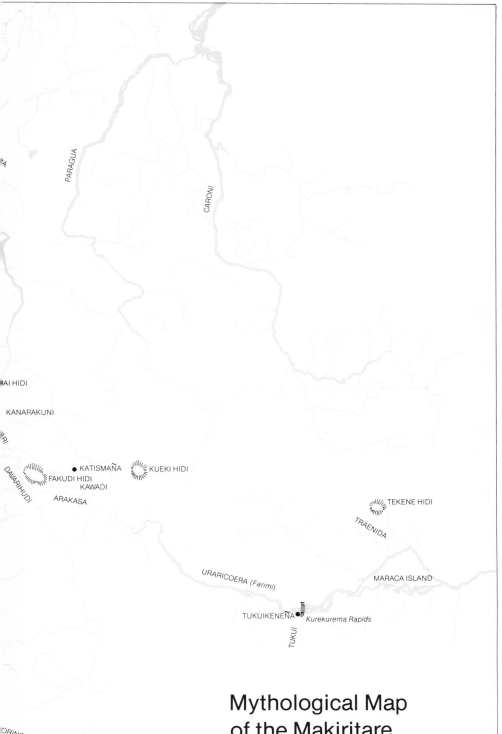

PARAGUA

CARONI

A

AI HIDI

KANARAKUNI

RI

DAVARIHUDI

●KATISMAÑA

FAKUDI HIDI

KAWADI

ARAKASA

KUEKI HIDI

TEKENE HIDI

TRAENIDA

URARICOERA *(Farimi)*

MARACA ISLAND

TUKUIKENEÑA●

Kurekurema Rapids

TUKUI

ORINOCO

Mythological Map
of the Makiritare